# Nature and Natural Areas in Canada's Capital : an introductory guide for the Ottawa - Hull area

## by Daniel F. Brunton

**The Ottawa Citizen**
in co-operation with
**The Ottawa Field-Naturalists' Club,**
Ottawa, Ontario

**Editing and design**
Hilary Crane

**Cover illustration**
Ben Babelowsky

**Cover design and production**
Victor Prochazka Jr.

**Canadian Cataloguing in Publication Data**
*Brunton, Daniel F. (Daniel Francis), 1948 -*
*Nature and natural areas in Canada's capital*

*Includes index.*
*ISBN 0-9690251-3-0*

*1. Botany--National Capital Region (Ont. and Quebec). 2. Zoology--*
*National Capital Region (Ont. and Quebec). 3. Natural areas--Nation-*
*al Capital Region (Ont. and Quebec). I. Ottawa Field-Naturalists'*
*Club. II. Title*

*QH106.2.O5B78 1988   581.909713'84   C88-090155-1*

Dedicated to the men and women at the National Museum of Natural Sciences who have made such an important contribution to our knowledge of the natural history of Canada's Capital, in commemoration of the Museum's 75th anniversary
and
to Joni, David and all the other children for whom we hold the natural world and its wonders in trust.

# Preface

When **Paddy Sherman** moved to Ottawa to take up duties as publisher of *The Ottawa Citizen* he was struck by the contrast between Ottawa and his native British Columbia in regards to the physical environment and the animals that inhabit it. He had enjoyed the material that was available in coastal British Columbia to help people identify and understand its natural features. When his search for comparable material here came up empty, Sherman decided to do something about it. In 1985 he contacted The Ottawa Field-Naturalists' Club. The Club has been studying and documenting the natural history of this area for over a century and it is the oldest and largest such organization in Canada. While discussions were held within the Club during its 1979 centennial celebrations regarding the possibility of publishing a 'Naturalists' Guide to the Ottawa District', time and circumstances prevented it.

From late 1985 into early 1986 discussions were held between officials of the Ottawa Field-Naturalists and *The Ottawa Citizen*. The concept for this book developed from those discussions. *The Ottawa Citizen* agreed to underwrite the costs of preparation and production; the Ottawa Field-Naturalists would provide the natural history expertise and the necessary technical audits of the process and products. The Ottawa Field-Naturalists selected me to prepare the manuscript, under contract to *The Ottawa Citizen*, and the project was on.

While of necessity the majority of the book is based on existing documentation, I was able to visit many of the areas discussed to renew a familiarity obtained from previous studies in the Ottawa area. This book, then, draws heavily on the documentation of natural history information by Ottawa Field-Naturalists' Club members over the years. It is supplemented by my own field experience in the Ottawa District over the last 25 years.

Four individuals undertook to review the entire manuscript for technical accuracy. The effort and time given by Drs. **Ron Bedford, Bill Gummer, Clarence Frankton**, and **Karen McIntosh** greatly improved the final product. Selected portions of the manuscript were also reviewed by a number of individuals with specialized expertise or concerns. Several individuals with the National Capital Commission, including **Stewart Hamill** and **Heather Wilson**, reviewed sections pertinent to the Commission. Similarly, **Donald Cuddy** examined sections relating to areas of concern for the Ontario Ministry of Natural Resources, as did **Laura Cole** of the Mississippi Valley Conservation Authority and **Leanne Kane** of the Rideau Valley Conservation Authority. **Bruce Di Labio** of Ottawa offered valuable criticisms of the sections discussing bird information as did **F.R. Cook** and **B. Coad** of the National Museum of Natural Sciences for reptiles and amphibians, and fish, respectively. **Joyce Reddoch** of Gloucester reviewed the factual content of several areas.

The majority of the pen and ink sketches were provided by the National Museum of Natural Sciences. My sincere thanks to Director **Alan Emery,** to Head of Publishing **Bonnie Livingstone** and to the various curators - notably **I.M. Brodo, H. Ouellet, F.R. Cook** and **B. Coad** - for their help and encouragement. Much of this went well beyond the call of duty. While many of the illustrations were from previously published sources (Cook's *Introduction to Canadian Amphibians and Reptiles*, McAllister and Coad's *Fishes of Canada's National Capital Region* and Godfrey's *Brids of Canada*), the botanical sketches were not. Artist **Sally Gadd** prepared these under the supervision of **J.M. Gillett**. They are a portion of the illustrations drawn for Dr. Gillett's up-coming *Flora of Gatineau Park*. In addition to the National Museum material, use of mammal sketches prepared for R.L. Peterson's *Mammals* *of Eastern Canada* by the Royal Ontario Museum was generously permitted by **Dr. Peterson.**

It is a pleasure and an honour to be incorporating the work of such exceptional artists as **John Crosby, Charles Douglas, Karl Pogany** and **Terry Shortt.**

Photographic materials were obtained from a number of individuals, as noted with each illustration. The graphics were prepared by **Marc Guertin** of Ottawa.

The concept for this book was worked out with a number of people in the Ottawa Field-Naturalists, most prominent being Presidents **Frank Pope** and **Bill Gummer.** **Ben Babelowsky,** *The Ottawa Citizen*'s Director of Public Relations, Promotions and Educational Services, provided administrational supervision of the project.

It fell to **Hilary Crane,** Special Projects Co-ordinator at *The Ottawa Citizen*, to perform the hands-on editorial work as well as the million and one logistical tasks required to blend the text and the illustrations into a smooth, effective product. This was complex and demanding and she deserves sincere thanks for her skillful and effective labours.

Similarly, the effort of my wife, **Karen McIntosh**, must be acknowledged. Not only did she assist me in the field in many of the sites described, but she helped in the development of the concept for the book, with the selection of illustrative material and with the preparation of the index; she also read the entire manuscript twice. Her wise and careful insights and suggestions run all through this work, as they do in so many other projects.

And finally, there would have been no book were it not for the initiative and interest of Southam Newspaper Group president **Paddy Sherman**. To him goes a hearty measure of the credit for the project.

*Daniel F. Brunton*
*Ottawa, March 1988*

# CONTENTS

# Further Information

# INTRODUCTION

There are countless wonderful places for the naturalist or nature-oriented person to visit in Canada's Capital. Some are exotic relicts of a landscape that dominated the Capital thousands of years ago and now is gone. Others are unexplored neighbourhood woodlots and wetlands that one could easily pass by. In this book I'm going to identify and discuss a few of these areas to give readers a "springboard" into the natural world.

The quantity of information that has been prepared on the natural features and natural areas of the Capital would literally fill many metres of library shelf space. So what, you might reasonably ask, will this book add to that? My intention is to add only a little new information ; my main purpose is to help the reader get through to the answers and opportunities offered here without being swamped by this mountain of paper. I want to help the uninitiated to recognize the most common plants and animals in the Capital and to begin to understand how habitats - natural neighbourhoods - are critical to the lives of wild plants and animals and important to our understanding of both.

And for those readers who find this particularly appealing, who find that the natural world is a new and exciting one of which they wish to know more, I'll be offering directions to more detailed information. You will be pleasantly surprised to see how much help is available, not just self-help but assistance from a variety of talented individuals, institutions and organizations.

There is so much in the natural world of the Capital that I cannot hope to cover all of it in one small volume. I can, however, bring some of the fascinating creatures, plants and landscapes that inhabitat the area to your attention.

It is important to remember that the natural world is the bottom line for all of us. Ultimately, plants, animals and humans depend on a naturally functioning world for continued survival on planet earth. That the features that make up this ecosystem are also interesting, beautiful and useful to us is an added bonus. It is important for us to understand how this system works for plants and animals since it is our system too.

## Scope of the Book

In the early days of natural history investigation in the Capital it was decided to identify a distinct study area within which the fledgling naturalist community could concentrate its effort. Thus, in 1879 The Ottawa Field-Naturalists' Club identified the Ottawa District as being a 25 mile wide circle centered on Parliament Hill. That was considered to be a reasonable limit of range for a day's investigations on foot ! By 1895, with better roads and a wider system of railway routes to choose from, the Field-Naturalists expanded that to a 60 mile wide circle. That area, "metricized" in 1981 to a 100 km-wide circle, has served as the limit for the Ottawa District ever since.

**Canada's Capital**, the area considered in this book, is the same 100 km-wide circle.

In addition to this geographic limit, we have to consider how broadly we can examine the diversity within the natural world. There are over 1500 species of vascular plants, hundreds of species of non-vascular plants, 300 species of birds, thousands of species of insects...and so on...in the Capital. To keep all of this within reasonable limits in an introductory guide, I have considered only the most striking and

characteristic plants and animals that the casual observer might encounter. Directions to sources for more detailed discussions can be found in the "Additional Sources and Assistance" section.

## The Landscape

The Capital is situated in one of the most interesting ecological crossroads in eastern Canada. Because of the history of the area and its geographic position, a whole complex of ecological systems has influenced and continues to influence its natural environment. The greatest single factor in determining the landscape variation of the Capital, however, is the existence of the Canadian Shield.

There are two quite different regions in the Capital. The vast upland of Canadian Shield rock on the Quebec side of the Ottawa River and in a large area in western Ottawa-Carleton is distinctly different from the flatter lowlands of the Ottawa River plain and the rest of the area on the Ontario side of the Ottawa River. The Shield is composed of ancient, very hard, acidic rock. The ice sheets of the Wisconsin glacier scraped away the soil that covered it and little has developed in the 100 or so centuries since. The steep slopes and erosion resistant bedrock have contributed to severe disruption of the drainage system here, resulting in the formation of many large and small lakes and innumerable creeks and streams. In the lowlands a younger, softer rock, much of which is calcareous (limy) or non-acid, underlies lake and sea deposits. This has resulted in the development of deep, rich soil. It is easier to build upon, has fewer, broader waterways and far greater agricultural potential than the Shield lands. So it is that the lowlands are more developed and have less natural landscape remaining.

These combinations of soil, topography, developmental history and drainage have had a profound effect on the plants and animals that live on the Shield lands and in the lowlands. The two areas are sufficiently ecologically different that it is possible to find organisms that are common in Gatineau Park, for example, but are very rare or even unknown on the Ontario side of the Ottawa River. This adds a tremendous richness to the diversity of the Capital.

We are situated here within a forest region that is transitional between the cool, coniferous-dominated Boreal Forest Region to the north and the warmer, broadleaf-dominated Deciduous Forest Region to the south. Each forest region has a distinctive association of plants and animals which depend on the ecological characteristics of that area for their continued prosperity. The Great Lakes - St. Lawrence Forest Region, as ours is called, contains elements of both of the others. This gives us the opportunity to see how locally varying ecological conditions favour one or the other sets of plants and animals in the Capital. No one who lives here year-round would deny that winters are long and cold with lots of snow. This is important, not only for those who like to skate, ski or toboggan, but for the way it helps define what can and cannot live here. Many plants and animals cannot withstand significantly more winter cold than Canada's Capital offers and so are found no further north. Others, more surprisingly perhaps, must have lots of snow and cold if they are to reproduce successfully and so they prosper here. This contributes to the diversity of the Capital area.

So too do our wetlands. The Capital area is rich in waterways, dominated by the mighty Ottawa River that divides the Ottawa Valley and serves as the provincial boundary. It and other rivers have offered important avenues for plant and animal migration for thousands of years since the last ice age... just as they did for human immigrants several thousand years ago and for later historical figures such as Samuel de Champlain, Etienne Brule, the LaVerendryes, David Thompson and Simon Fraser. Our rivers have helped to shape the human history of the Capital and the nation, just as they have helped to shape the natural history of the Ottawa Valley. Other wetland areas, including bogs, swamps, marshes and lakes, provide distinctive habitats for a wide variety of wildlife and plant life, including a number of provincially and even nationally significant species.

For you or me, perhaps the most important landscape is the one near our home. If you do not live along the Ottawa or Gatineau Rivers or at the edge of the Canadian Shield or by a relict forest, you should not think that your backyard is not an important part of the complex landscape that makes up the Capital. Many of the plants, animals and situations discussed in this book can be seen in a backyard, from a high-rise balcony or on the lawns of the Parliament Buildings!

## Using this Book

There are a number of things you can do that will help you get the most out of this book. Obviously, the more you know about natural history the better. Without previous experience, however, you can still get lots out of it.

Firstly, I suggest you read about the different habitats that preface the treatment of individual plants and animals. A description follows the page of photographs of typical examples of each habitat. habitat . This should help to "pigeon-hole" different landscape types. A quick review of the treatments of typical plants and animals in each may also help to define what that habitat looks and sounds like. Next, I would suggest that you look over the list of example areas identified with each habitat and select familiar ones, areas close to home,or areas that simply sound interesting. The "Places to See" section of the book will tell you more about each place and how to get the most out of it at a particular time of year. You would be well advised to read the "Do's and Don'ts" section to see what considerations apply to the area or areas that you are thinking of visiting. Then, away you go! Afterwards, if you wish to know more about some of the plants or animals or landscapes that you experienced, consult the "Further Information" section.

Some readers may find that this book provides a useful checklist of interesting areas to be visited one by one over the course of a year (or years). Others may wish to refer to it for more information on an area they already know well. Still others may wish to identify unknown plants and animals of particular habitats that they have encountered in their travels in the Capital area. All of these and more are worthwhile uses of the book and will help the reader to enter more deeply into the fascinating natural world around us.

A word of caution : there are literally thousands of different plant and animal species in the Capital, but I have space for only common and representative examples in each habitat discussion. If you encounter a plant or animal that you cannot identify by this guide, you should at least have an idea of its habitat and perhaps will have been introduced to an associated species. That will help you if you really want to get to the bottom of things and go on to consult the "Further Information" section. When you have visited a variety of places through the seasons and feel that you have a pretty good understanding at the level I have presented them, you might join one of the naturalists clubs in the Capital area or look into more advanced reading material.

There is a large and active naturalist community in the Capital and across the Ottawa Valley; they are always keen to help others explore the natural world. Being in the field with an experienced naturalist is perhaps THE best way of all to learn about natural history and its varied, fascinating elements.

# HABITATS

Every plant and animal on earth requires a certain set of ecological conditions to exist if it too is to exist. Some of these conditions are very general, such as the availability of air and water. Others are quite specific, as with an insect that depends totally on one species of plant for its food and shelter. When all of these elements are viewed together they form distinct associations of plant, animal and landscape features. These *ecological neighbourhoods*, if you will, are called HABITATS .

Since each represents a distinctive set of plants and animals, only a limited number of species can be found in any particular habitat. That is of great help to anyone wishing to sort out the endless variety of wild lifeforms into manageable-sized units. If habitats can be identified, experience and research can tell us what plants and animals might be expected in each.

Habitats vary almost as widely as the number of plants and animals found within them. The underside of a small boulder, for example, could be the habitat for hundreds or even thousands of microscopic plants and animals, while the vast arctic ice-pack provides habitat for a relatively few Polar Bear and Ringed Seal. Developing precise habitat descriptions is important for scientific investigation of the natural world but is beyond the scope of this book. I have identified broad habitat groupings that are likely to be familiar to most readers. These are broader than would be found in technical analyses of vegetation, but this is a liberty that I have taken so that readers are not overwhelmed by unfamiliar terms and descriptions.

The seven habitat groups that the landscape of Canada's Capital has been divided into are as follows:

**(1) UPLAND FOREST (Page 17)** - tree-covered land where the ground is never (or rarely) covered with standing water. The soil is usually a form of clay, sand or silt and can vary from moist to very dry. White Pine stands and Sugar Maple forests are good examples of this habitat.

**(2) MEADOWS & BARRENS (Page 35)** - unforested lands, often found along the edge of forested areas, that are covered with young shrubbery and sapling growth ; also includes open grasslands and bare rock flats. The soil can be similar to that of Upland Forest habitat, or can be thin or even absent. This habitat is often very dry. Alvars, cliff-faces, relict prairies and raspberry thickets offer some interesting examples of this habitat.

**(3) FARM & COUNTRY (Page 51)** - open crop land or pastures that are currently (or recently) cultivated to produce agricultural products. The natural vegetation has largely been replaced by non-native weed species, crops and pasture grasses. Corn fields, sod farms, sheep pasture and feed lots are examples of this.

**(4) URBAN LANDSCAPE (Page 67)** - heavily built-up, artificially developed landscapes within the cities and suburbs ; trees and shrubs (often non-native species) are selectively established throughout. Ground conditions are extremely variable. Examples of this habitat include city parks, backyard bird feeders, road allowances through subdivisions and ornamental gardens.

**(5) FORESTED WETLAND (Page 79)** - tree-covered land where the ground is covered in standing water on a permanent or seasonal basis. The soil is often muddy, silty or even made up entirely of only partially decayed organic material. It varies from wet to saturated and is exemplified by Silver Maple swamps, Black Spruce - Larch bogs, cedar swamps and ash swamps.

**(6) OPEN WETLAND (Page 91)** - non-forested land that is permanently wet or flooded to a depth of about 1 metre or more, often along major waterways. The ground is sandy, silty or clay-based in most areas ; peatlands of partially decayed organic material in bogs and fens are exceptions. Cat-tail marshes, alder thickets and sedge meadows are other examples of this habitat.

**(7) LAKES & RIVERS (Page 107)** - permanently flooded areas, often to depths of many meters of flowing water, with no standing vegetation present. A vast array of floating and submerged aquatic plant species are found here. Beaver ponds, creeks, river rapids and lakes are typical of this habitat.

In each of the following habitat treatments I describe typical plants and animals through illustrations as well as words. I use the common names of animals, as these are firmly established in the natural history literature. For plants, however, the scientific names are also included, since many have poorly defined common names.

14

Upland Forest

**Sugar Maple Woods, Kanata**
*(D.F. Brunton)*

# UPLAND FOREST

When Samuel de Champlain first looked upon the Capital area well over three centuries ago it must have seemed to be an unending sea of trees. And indeed it was. Wherever the land was reasonably dry, upland forests grew. These forests varied considerably in composition, depending on the ground conditions available to them, their history and site characteristics. Red, White and Jack Pine forests covered the deep, dry sands along the Ottawa River in such places as Constance Bay, on the site of the Ottawa International Airport and at Baie Noir. Massive pines would also have dominated dry ridges and slopes, as well as being commonly scattered throughout the hardwoods across the Capital and especially in the Gatineau Hills. Maple forest was by far the most common upland forest habitat , although the taller, conspicuous crowns of ancient White Pine would have given the appearance of dominance by that tree. It is a popular misconception that the Capital and the Ottawa Valley were wall-to-wall pine in the early days. This was only a local condition of sand plains and shores.

A hardwood habitat of Sugar Maple, Beech, Yellow Birch and Red Maple still dominates areas of richer, deeper soils that are relatively undisturbed. When natural disturbance takes place on a large scale, however, the established order of things is drastically altered. A mature maple forest, often with groves of Eastern Hemlock and White Cedar in it, permits little sunlight to reach the forest floor. A fire opens up this canopy, flooding the ground level with sunlight and allowing opportunities for a multitude of new plant species to develop. Fast growing trees like Trembling Aspen , White Birch and Balsam Fir, which all require an abundance of light, spring up in these openings. A period of tremendous diversity and activity for plants and animals is initiated. This is the habitat of the Moose, the White-tailed Deer and a myriad of smaller creatures. As the successful early-growing species mature, however, they are overtaken by the more slowly developing tree species that dominated the site before it was renewed. They thrive in the slight shade of these 'pioneers' . Sugar Maple, by its ability to shade out all but the very slow growing Eastern Hemlock, becomes the dominant once more on richer sites. Old age, however, will encourage its vulnerability to disease and fire and will prepare it for yet another renewal. And so it goes ... birth, death and rebirth.

Upland forests in the Capital are particularly attractive in the spring and fall. This is especially so in maple forests. Before the shade from the fully developed canopy stifles the supply of life-giving sunlight, a spectacular bloom of wildflowers carpets the forest floor. Even the names of these flowers conjure up bright and lively images ... Spring-beauty, Trout-lily, Starflower , Wake-robin. The fall colours of upland forests, with the reds, yellows and browns of hardwoods mixing with the deep green of conifers, are justifiably famous. It is the cold nights and shorter days of early fall that help to break down the green pigment in broad-leafed tree leaves, permitting the rainbow hues of other leaf chemicals to show through. A few weeks later these leaves will fall and will help to provide an insulating blanket over the forest floor through the cold months of winter. Eventually they will decay, contributing to the on-going enrichment of the soil and providing nutrients to future generations of wildflowers and trees.

It is the upland forest that first convinced white men to settle in this area. The abundance of pine and the power from harnessing the rapids on the Ottawa and tributary rivers drew the first industrialists and loggers here almost 200 years ago. Forestry remains an important industry in the Capital, although our forest resources are greatly reduced from former years.

What Champlain witnessed is still here, but only a fraction of the great upland forests that covered the Capital remains ; the larger portion has been transformed into housing, farmland or industrial development. I think Champlain would be amazed at the changes. While we still enjoy many of the bounties of these lands, much is permanently changed. Passenger Pigeons will never again feed in the beech trees of Rockcliffe Park, Beechwood and the Glebe, nor will Cougar stalk White-tailed Deer along shrubby valleys in the Gatineau Hills. The howl of the Timber Wolf is now so rare that the ultimate loss of this magnificent mammal seems assured. Fortunately, we have maintained natural areas of upland forest in parts of the Greenbelt, in the Marlborough Forest, in Gatineau Park and elsewhere for residents and visitors alike to experience and appreciate.

## Some Places to Visit

**Gatineau Park**
- walking trails from Champlain Lookout (rich maple forests).
- walking trail south from the Mackenzie King Estate along Mulvihill Creek (mature maple - hemlock forest; spring wildflowers).
- hiking trail from Black Lake to King Mountain summit (variety of developing broadleaf and coniferous forest types).

**Tache Gardens Woods**
- trail west from Hull Jail (rich, rocky forest of maple, Beech and Eastern Hemlock, with interesting southern flora).

**Wychwood**
- side roads along river shore (mature White Pine forest).

**Mill of Kintail**
- walking trail through maple woods (young and mature Sugar Maple - Beech forests; rich spring wildflower display).

**The Burnt Lands**
- south of Highway 44 at the County line (upland cedar - spruce forest with rich spring and fall flora).

**Britannia Conservation Area**
- west side of Mud Lake (White Pine stand, young maple forest).
- south side of the wood (scrubby ash - elm - pine forest; migrating woodland birds).

## Carlington Woods
- recreational pathway above ski hill (young hardwoods on rocky out-crop; migrating woodland birds).

## Green's Creek Conservation Area
- northwest corner of National Capital Commission nursery, Innis Road (mature Eastern Hemlock in clay ravines).

## Lower Duck Island
- boat to island (mature Hackberry stand and other southern plant species).

## Mer Bleue Conservation Area
- Dolman Ridge trails east of Anderson Road (young poplar - birch forest with diverse ground plant communities).

## Pine Grove Trail
- trail off Davidson Road (young White Pine stand; winter bird feeder).

**Staghorn Clubmoss** *(Lycopodium clavatum)*
- low, sprawling plant named for its branching pattern resembling a deer's antlers; a fern ally that produces fruiting bodies filled with tiny yellow spores on bare stems above the leaves; found commonly in dry, sandy or rocky ground in young forests.

**Rattlesnake Fern** *(Botrychium virginianum )*
- a small, dark green fern (like a miniature Bracken) with one erect branch carrying only spore cases; one of the grape-ferns, so named for their grape-like spore case clusters; common in cool, moist woods (hardwoods and conifers).

**Ground Pine** *(Lycopodium dendroideum)*
- like a tiny, dark green evergreen tree except for the tell-tale spore cases extending from the tips of the branches; actually a fern ally; common in mature, shady hardwoods and mixed forests in sandy and loamy soil.

**Evergreen Woodfern** *(Dryopteris intermedia)*
- a delicate woodland fern with finely divided leaves covered by dot-like fruiting bodies beneath and distinctive chaffy scales on the lower part of the stems; grows in clumps in drier ground in young to mature hardwoods and mixed forest.

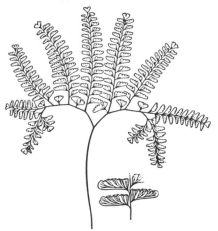

**Maidenhair Fern** *(Adiantum pedatum)*
- a delicate beauty, with soft, green drooping leaves and leaflets contrasting with blackish stems; forms large patches on sandy or loamy knolls in mature maple forest across the Gatineau Hills and (uncommonly) in Ottawa-Carleton.

**Eastern Hemlock** *(Tsuga canadensis)*
- shaggy, dark green conifer with short, flat needles (leaves); large numbers of tiny cones produced amongst its branches; forms stands in cool, moist sites in maple forests and shaded slopes; offers important winter shelter for deer and other wildlife.

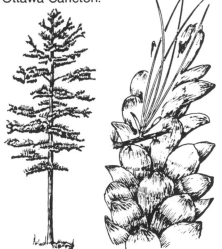

**White Pine** *(Pinus strobus)*
- a huge, magnificent tree of sandy, rocky ridges and drier knolls in forests throughout; can be told from other local pines by its 5 needles (leaves) in a bundle; its seed provides an important food source for wintering birds and small mammals.

**Bladder Sedge** *(Carex intumescens)*
- grass-like plant with lax, dark green leaves; seeds contained in small bladders (perigynia) grouped together near the top of the plant; found commonly in low spots in shady forest; one of over 100 sedge species in the Capital.

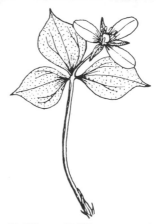

**Bluebead Lily** *(Clintonia borealis)*
- drooping, yellow flowers and (later) blue berries distinctive on a single stalk from fleshy, dark green leaves; a common species of acidic soil in partly to heavily shaded coniferous and mixed forest, especially in the Gatineau Hills.

**White Trillium** *(Trillium grandiflorum)*
- spectacular white-flowered spring wildflower; the provincial emblem of Ontario; locally abundant, slow growing perennial lily (when not picked!) in hardwood forests; very common in mature maple forests in the Gatineau Hills.

**Trout-lily** *(Erythronium americanum)*
- one of the first common spring wildflowers to emerge in spring; a single drooping, spotted, yellow flower above mottled green leaves; locally abundant in hardwoods everywhere; all but disappears when the leaves wither away in early summer.

**Pink Lady's-slipper** *(Cypripedium acaule)*
- large, exotic-looking pink flower supported by a straight, bare stem above two broad hairy leaves at the ground; a plant of dry sandy or rocky acidic ground, though also found in wet mossy ground of bog forests.

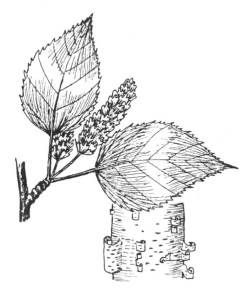

**Helleborine** *(Epipactis helleborine)*
- a thin spike of greenish-purple flowers above several narrow, dark green leaves on an upright stem; found commonly in moist, calcareous sites, usually under tree cover; the only non-native orchid in the Capital and still expanding its range.

**White Birch** *(Betula papyrifera)*
- small, fast growing hardwood tree with distinctive white, curling bark; usually found with aspen in dry, lighter soil where plenty of sunlight is available; produces vast quantities of seed in some years which contribute an important food source for wintering finches.

**Trembling Aspen** *(Populus tremuloides)*
- tall, thin, pale-barked tree of open, sandy or rocky dry sites; intolerant of shade and soon replaced by other tree species; named for fluttering of long-stemmed leaves in even gentle breezes.

**Spring-beauty** *(Claytonia caroliniana)*
- early spring wildflower with delicate,pink-striped white flowers and long, tapering green leaves; found commonly in mature maple forests in loamy soil in stands that may be a century or more in age; all traces of the plant are gone by mid-summer.

**Blue Cohosh** *(Caulophyllum gigateum var. thalictroides)*
- newly unfurling leaves and stem show a distinctive purple colour in moist, early spring hardwood forests in rich, loamy soil; small purple and yellow flowers give way to groups of purple berries shortly after the forest canopy has filled out.

**Wild Sarsaparilla** *(Aralia nudicaulis)*
- three-branched with dark green leaf segments and clumps of pale flowers and (later) dark, hard berries on separate branches from leaves; dry to moist woodland sites; unusually shade tolerant, persisting even beneath Eastern Hemlock groves.

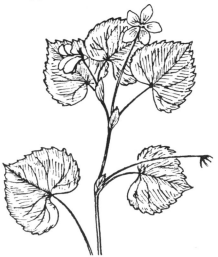

**Yellow Violet** *(Viola pubescens)*
- small, weak-stemmed, pale green plant; bright yellow flowers stand out against broad, usually downy leaves; grows commonly in light, sandy soil in open hardwoods; one of almost 20 species of violets in the Capital.

**Indian Pipe** *(Monotropa uniflora)*
- ghostly-white stem and flowers result from total absence of green chlorophyll; plant obtains nutrients from decaying vegetation, through a partnership with subterranean fungi ; found on knolls and drier sites in hardwoods.

**Shinleaf** *(Pyrola elliptica)*
- small woodland plant with dish-like white flowers in a spike arising from a rosette of elliptic, leathery leaves; common in sandy soil and loam in young hardwoods and mixed forest; supposedly possessing herbal qualities.

**Fragrant Bedstraw** *(Galium triflorum)*
- matted, sprawling plant with whorls of six narrow leaves occurring regularly along the stem; clusters of tiny white flowers arise on separate branches; common in young hardwoods in moist to dry soils; formerly used to freshen hay mattresses because of its enduring fragrance.

**Starflower** *(Trientalis borealis)*
- one or two tiny, white, star-like flowers above a whorl of narrow, green leaves; single bare stem; grows commonly in light, moist, often acidic soil under coniferous and hardwoods forests alike.

**Whorled Aster** *(Aster acuminatus)*
- low plant with large, narrow, dark green leaves in a whorl (or nearly so) under a branching head of small, many-petalled flowers; abundant on lighter, dry slopes in hardwoods and mixed forest in the Gatineau Hills; flowers in late summer and fall.

**Large-leaved Aster** (*Aster macrophyllus* )
- large, heart-shaped basal leaves, usually growing in sizeable, mostly sterile patches with only occasional flowering stems of white or pinkish flowers; prefers sunny sites in sandy or rocky ground throughout the Capital.

**Sugar Maple** (*Acer saccharum*)
- a magnificent hardwood tree with leaves like those of Red Maple but with more rounded lobes; dominates most other trees in upland sites; the model for the leaf on our national flag and the main producer of maple syrup and hardwood timber in eastern Canada.

**Broad-winged Hawk**
- crow-sized raptor with broad white bands across its short, black tail; common breeding bird of hardwood forest edges, hunting from trees, poles and wires for frogs, snakes and small mammals ; most commonly seen in summer in the Gatineau Hills.

**Northern Goshawk**
- large, long-tailed, powerful hawk; adults evenly blue-gray above, pale gray below; young are brown and streaked; a local breeder here but occasionally fairly common migrant and winter resident; preys on grouse, rabbits and other larger species.

**Whip-poor-will**
- drably-coloured, nocturnal bird named for its distinctive "*whip-poor-will*" call; very hard to see except on back roads in young hardwoods or mixed forest at night; feeds on insects that are caught on the wing; migrates far to the south each winter.

**Great Horned Owl**
- very large, nocturnal resident; a rich brown in colour with distinctive ear tufts; looks much like a large cat high in a tree; an earlier breeder, with eggs in the nest by February and young fledged by mid May; feeds mostly on small mammals.

**Ruffed Grouse**
- chicken-sized reddish-brown or gray bird with a broad, banded tail; drumming of courting male (like a rubber ball falling on a hardwood floor) is a familiar spring sound in young hardwoods and mixed forests throughout the Capital.

**Northern Flicker**
- chunky, brown and yellow woodpecker; found in open woodlands foraging for insects in tree bark crevices and along limbs, or grubbing on fallen logs or in the ground; a common breeding species in the Capital.

## Eastern Wood-Pewee
- a plain, olive-brown flycatcher best identified by its *"peee-a-wee"* call; common breeder and persistent singer in hardwood forests throughout the Capital; hawks for insects (flying out from a perch); migrates south each fall.

## Black-capped Chickadee
- boisterous, black, gray and white bundle of continuous activity; a common woodland resident, noisily foraging for insect larvae, seeds and other bits of food; a delightful winter bird feeder visitor, readily taught to take seeds from the hand.

## Blue Jay
- distinctive, raucous, bright-blue bird of mixed and hardwood forest; a common resident and close relative of the crow; usually paired up throughout the year; will readily accept sunflower seeds and suet at winter bird feeders.

## White-breasted Nuthatch
- small, busy, gray and white bird of hardwood forests; a year-round resident known as "the up-side down bird" for its habit of walking *down* trees in search of seeds and insects in bark crevices; nests in holes in large hardwood trees.

**Veery**
- warm-brown coloured, delicate thrush, known for its fluty descending "*vera-vera-vera-ver*" song; a common bird of young hardwoods in summer and a common spring migrant.

**Northern Oriole (formerly Baltimore Oriole)**
- a spectacular orange and black blackbird (females are a plain yellow-orange); prefers edge of hardwoods and is commonly seen along rivers, roadways and clearings; builds a deep, sac-like nest suspended precariously from the tip of a long tree limb.

**Red-eyed Vireo**
- a plain, greenish-white bird; one of our most common upland species but seldom seen high up in the canopy of hardwood forests; persistent singer throughout the summer and a common migrant; an insect--eating bird.

**Rose-breasted Grosbeak**
- beautiful black and white bird with a patch of bright red on the throat (females and immatures are brown and streaked); found in hardwood forests throughout the Capital, singing its long, warbling song (like a robin in a hurry) from high in the trees.

**Evening Grosbeak**
- noisy, handsome black, yellow and white finch; rarely seen in summer but often common in large flocks in the winter; known as "greedies" by feeder operators for their appetite for sunflower seeds; otherwise feed on nuts, seeds and twlg buds.

**Dark-eyed Junco**
- small, plain sparrow with distinctive gray hood and flashing white outer tail feathers; common early spring and late fall migrant and uncommon ground breeder in coniferous forest in the Gatineau Hills; winters in small numbers.

**American Goldfinch**
- tiny, musical yellow and black bird of scrubby woods and woodland edges; often called wild canary; common breeder and occasionally common winter resident (when birch and cedar seed crops are large); often travels in mixed flocks with other winter finches.

**Eastern Chipmunk**
- perky, pale-brown ground squirrel with distinctive black and white striped back; loud *"tock"* call note a common sound in summer hardwoods; eats nuts, berries and seeds, carrying extra food away in large cheek pouches; hibernates through the winter.

## Red Squirrel
- boisterous, reddish-brown tree squirrel of coniferous, mixed and occasionally hardwood forests; eats just about anything, but stores pine cones, nuts, mushrooms, etc. in caches for the winter; lives year-round in a large leaf, twig and grass nest .

## Porcupine
- a very large blackish rodent that has many painfully sharp quills within its fur; found in various woodlands where it eats the bark from almost any species of tree; largely nocturnal; slow-moving, fearless habit makes it vulnerable to road traffic.

## Deer Mouse
- a tiny mammal with light brown fur above, large round ears and a long tail; the most common woodland mouse in the District; active year-round and nocturnal, searching for seeds, nuts and other plant foods; often forages in buildings in woodlands.

## Snowshoe Hare
- a large rabbit with brown fur in summer, white in winter; named for its large feet which are well suited for winter travel; mostly in mixed and coniferous forests in wilder areas of the District but also found within cities.

## Red-backed Salamander
- a small (about 100 mm) blackish amphibian, usually with a reddish-brown stripe along its back; locally common in low, mixed and hardwood forests under logs, in leaf litter, etc.; feeds (at night) on worms and other invertebrates.

## Gray Treefrog
- a small, gray, brown or green frog (changes skin colour to suit the background); its long, slow trill is a frequent sound in mid-summer hardwood and mixed forests across the Capital; inconspicuous appearance make it hard to find.

## Wood Frog
- a small, brownish frog with a black "lone ranger" mask across its eyes; one of the first amphibian to sing each spring, giving a series of duck-like "*quack*" calls from temporary pools in a variety of upland forests; a common animal in the Capital.

Meadows & Barrens

**Overgrown pastureland, Nepean**
*(W.K. Gummer)*

# MEADOWS & BARRENS

The upland areas of Canada's Capital will, given enough time and protection from disturbance, develop into mature forests. Nature is not like that in reality, however, as various factors interrupt the maturing process. Fires, windstorms, insect outbreaks and the like were important agents of forest renewal in prehistoric times. They remain important in those few areas where natural processes are left more or less to their own devices. Man is the biggest manipulator of the landscape today; we have both intentionally and incidentally introduced plants, animals and circumstances that have permanently altered the natural state of things in the Capital.

Following severe disturbance to a forested area usually and unfortunately called the "destruction" of that growth, renewal begins with a vigour unseen at the site for decades. Sunlight, which is the basis for life in the plant world, floods down onto the ground. With the enrichment of the soil by the nutrients released from the decaying material of the former forest cover, this flood of sunlight sets the stage for a rush of growth. A diverse plant and animal community develops and changes as this rejuvenation occurs. Depending on the ground conditions and history at a particular site, this renewal can take many forms.

Abandoned pasture overgrowing with elm, ash, birch, poplar or cedar saplings is perhaps the most common example of this habitat in the Capital. It is an artificially created situation following the removal of forest cover and subsequent tilling of the soil for a period of years. These areas support a large number of non-native plant and animal species that thrive in disturbed openings at the expense of native species.

Much of the Meadows and Barrens habitat represents rehabilitating agricultural lands that can no longer support an economical operation. This is brought home with particular force for me when I come across a depression in a woodland clearing that marks where a home once stood. A large Lilac bush or straggly clusters of hardy cultivars stand out as silent testimony to the hopes and failed aspirations of the homestead's long-gone and anonymous residents.

Probably the most common *native* example of Meadows and Barrens habitat in the Capital is the upland thicket. It usually comprises a mixture of Beaked Hazel, Red-osier Dogwood, various raspberries, Staghorn Sumac and hawthorn. Such areas are often along the edge of young forest growth. They are alive with the colour and form of a myriad of flowers and fruits from the many shrubs and non-woody plants that thrive in these protected, sunny sites. This in turn attracts a wide variety of small mammals and birds as well as larger creatures like the White-tailed Deer, the Black Bear and even the Moose. The latter two are found mostly in such sites in the Outaouais area.

Alvar, a spring-flooded, summer-droughted limestone plain with a distinctive vegetation and flora, is locally common in the Capital. It is found sparingly across Ontario, however, and is rare in Quebec. At the Burnt Lands near Almonte and at several sites in the Marlborough Forest, large alvar meadows have been naturally formed by generations of forest fires. Tree growth is limited at best in this demanding habitat and it has been regularly reduced by routinely occurring fires. This situation appears to

35

have been maintained since these areas first emerged from the cold waters of the Champlain Sea about 10,000 years ago. Some plants and animals at such sites in the Capital are otherwise unknown away from the Great Lakes shores, apparently stranded on these "islands" of suitable habitat.

The open rock barrens of cliff faces such as those along the southern edge of Gatineau Park are also sites for living relicts from prehistoric times. Here, as with the unusual alvar species, plants persist centuries after their elimination from all other sites in the Capital area. There are plants growing on ledges of Gatineau Park cliffs that quite literally have been there since Harp Seals were pupping on the pack-ice of the Champlain Sea below!

In clearings formed on deep sand deposits, relict prairies are occasionally found although blueberry and Bracken dominated vegetation is more typical. Animal life is restricted in this habitat which becomes exceptionally hot and dry in summer. It is dominated by species that are either dependent on fire to encourage their development or are very tolerant of it.

# Some Places to Visit

**Gatineau Park**
- Ramsay Lake (sandy fields and scrubland).
- Champlain Lookout (Eardley Escarpment cliffs and rock outcrops).

**Tache Gardens Woods**
- trail north from Lacasse Street (scrubby fields with rich weed flora).

**The Burnt Lands**
- south of Highway 44 at County line (mature alvar meadows in pine plantation).

**Constance Bay Sand Hills**
- fire road network (sandy clearing in planted pine forest for plants and butterflies).

**Marlborough Forest**
- along Flood Road (rich alvar meadows at north end).

**Carp Hills**
- Dolan Parkway (bedrock outcrops and scrubby clearings along the roadway).

**Carlington Woods**
- south of the recreational pathway (extensive open meadow of non-native plants).

**Mer Bleue Conservation Area**
- Dolman and Borthwick Ridge Trails (rich weedy fields in sand).

**Stony Swamp Conservation Area**
- east of Jack Pine Trail (disturbed meadows over limestone bedrock).
- Old Quarry Trail (scrubby meadows rich in non-native plants).

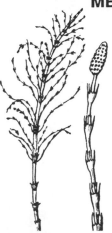

**Field Horsetail** *(Equisetum arvense)*
- thick, white, fertile stems with spore-laden "cones" on top emerge from the ground in early spring in large numbers; branched, green sterile shoots follow later; found commonly in open or partially shaded dry, sandy fields and edges.

**Marginal Shield Fern** *(Dryopteris marginalis)*
- robust, light green plant with many evergreen leaves arising from a tough, woody rhizome; spores are clustered in brown fruit dots on margins of leaf underside;found commonly on dry rock faces and outcrops.

**Fragile Fern** *(Cystopteris tenuis)*
- small, delicate fern with several pale green finely cut leaves in a small clump; found on shaded cliff ledges and rock outcrops; wilts quickly in drought or following frost, hence its common name.

**Polypody** *(Polypodium virginianum)*
- small, dark green evergreen fern arising from a blackish scaly rhizome with many large brown fruit dots on the underside of each leaf; common on shaded cliff faces, in crevices of rock pavement and even (rarely) on trees.

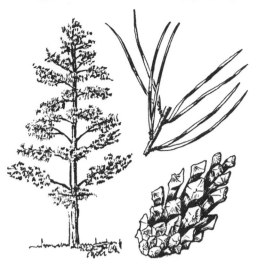

**Scot's Pine** *(Pinus sylvestris)*
- a small, introduced tree with reddish, scaly bark and needles in bunches of two; frequently planted in large numbers in old pastures, much to the detriment of other plant growth; occasionally spreads from such plantings.

**Bracken** *(Pteridium aquilinum)*
- tall, three-branched, much divided fern arising from a long, black rhizome; forms dense stands in open, dry, sandy or rocky ground; poisonous if eaten.

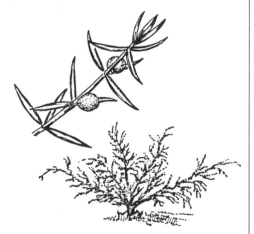

**Common Juniper** *(Juniperus communis)*
- low, sprawling evergreen shrub with short, spiny leaves and small, dry, blue berries; closely related to White Cedar; found commonly in dry, open sites on alvars, cliff tops, beaches, etc ; berries eaten by migratory and wintering birds.

**Canada Bluegrass** *(Poa compressa)*
- small, sparse grass with flattened stems, narrow leaves and slender heads of many flowers; found commonly in dry, rocky or sandy ground such as rock flats, beaches, roadsides and cliffs; very resistant to drought and cold.

**Pussy-willow** *(Salix discolor)*
- low, red-stemmed shrub with soft, fluffy flower heads emerging from bare twigs even before the snow has melted from the ground; plain, greenish leaves emerge later; found in low, wet meadows and edges.

**Curled Dock** *(Rumex crispus)*
- tall, robust plant with wavy-edged, narrow, green leaves along the stem and numerous dark brown seeds grouped on separate stalks; an introduction from Europe now found commonly in open, disturbed ground.

**Bindweed** *(Polygonum cilinode)*
- sprawling, vine-like buckwheat with large heart-shaped leaves along the stem; spikes of tiny white flowers are held on separate branches off the stem; forms huge mats in open, dry, rocky sites and weedy meadows.

**Sheep Sorrel** *(Rumex acetosella)*
- small plant with reddish stem and arrowhead-shaped leaves; a European introduction that is abundant in open, dry, disturbed ground; leaves have a refreshing, sharp taste, especially when one is thirsty.

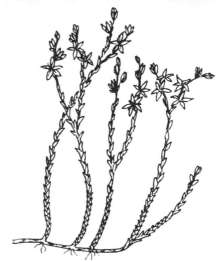

**Canada Anemone** *(Anemone canadensis)*
- low, pale green buttercup with broad, deeply divided leaves and large, cup-shaped white flowers; found in moist edges, meadows and rivershores in calcareous ground.

**Yellow Stonecrop** *(Sedum acre)*
- short, fleshy, pale green succulent growing in dense mats; bright yellow flowers form a brilliant carpet in mid summer on rocky hillsides, shores and rock flats where this garden escape has become established.

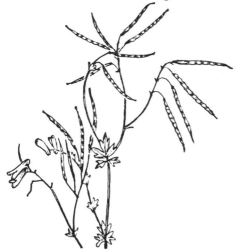

**Pale Harlequin** *(Corydalis sempervirens)*
- small, delicate, pale green plant with beautiful pink and yellow flowers blooming from early summer until fall; found on open granite outcrops and cliff tops in the Gatineau Hills and less commonly on acidic rock in Ottawa-Carleton.

**Early Saxifrage** *(Saxifraga virginiensis)*
- a cluster of tiny white flowers tops a straight, hairy stem from a rosette of thick, short, dark green leaves; in bloom in mid May on rock flats, cliff tops and outcrops; particularly common in the Gatineau Hills.

**Bristly Rose** *(Rosa acicularis)*
- low, sprawling shrub with dark green leaves, large pink flowers and densely spiny stems; common in dry, rocky or sandy areas; a widespread species in northern and western Canada (provincial flower of Alberta).

**Poison-ivy** *(Toxicodendron radicans)*
- low, trailing shrub (occasionally a vine) with shiny, dark green leaves in groups of three and separately branched clusters of white berries; common in open, rocky or sandy sites; oil from any part of the plant causes a skin rash and terrible itching for most people; "leaves in threes, let it be".

**Staghorn Sumac** *(Rhus typhina)*
- tall shrub (almost tree size) with "furry" branches, large, segmented, hairy leaves and a tall spike of hairy, deep-red berries; a close but inoffensive relative of Poison-ivy found in dry, sandy and rocky sites in the open.

**Fireweed** *(Epilobium angustifolium)*
- colourful plant with a narrow spike of pinkish-blue flowers above narrow green leaves along a straight, tall stem; amongst the first colonizers of newly disturbed, open, dry ground (such as burns); flowers in mid-summer.

**Velvetleaf Blueberry** *(Vaccinium myrtilloides)*
- low, much branched shrub with small, pale green, softly hairy leaves; flowers in late spring (pollinated by black flies) and produces large numbers of delicious blue berries in mid-summer; locally common in acidic, dry, open ground.

**Spreading Dogbane** *(Apocynum androsaemifolium)*
- tall, spreading plant with many elliptic, pale green leaves and small, drooping bell-like flowers; common in dry, open fields and shores; toxic to the touch for some people.

**Common St. John's-wort**
*(Hypericum perforatum)*
- shrubby plant with small, narrow leaves covered with translucent dots; red-spotted yellow flowers are conspicuous in late summer; a European introduction that is abundant in open dry meadows, rock flats and along roadways.

**Heal-all** *(Prunella vulgaris)*
- low, narrow-leaved plant with dense heads of blue flowers; a European introduction found in open, disturbed ground throughout developed areas as well as along woodland trails.

**Bluebell** *(Campanula rotundifolia)*
- a delicate, beautiful little plant with tiny, slender leaves and a disproportionately large bell shaped flower; usually grows in clumps; found in open rock of alvars, cliff tops, rock outcrops, etc.

**Gray Goldenrod** *(Solidago nemoralis)*
- narrow, gray-green, leafy plant with distinctively one-sided flowering head of many tiny yellow blooms; very common in dry,open, sterile ground of old pastures, on rock outcrops and in sandy areas; flowers in the fall.

**Fringed Blue Aster** *(Aster ciliolatus)*
- many-flowered, branched aster with long tapered, green leaves, each with winged petioles (leaf stems); flowers are pale blue with pale centers; found in open, dry, well-drained, usually acidic ground.

**Balsam Ragwort** *(Senecio pauperculus)*
- low, dark green plant with stems arising from clumps of deeply cut leaves; clusters of bright yellow flowers bloom in early summer; common (locally abundant) on dry calcareous ground and outcrops.

**American Woodcock**
- a squat, brown, bizarre looking shorebird; feeds (at night) by probing for worms with its exceptionally long bill; active at dawn and dusk in spring in open fields and woodland clearings, singing its beautiful, twinkling flight song.

**House Wren**
- tiny, plain brown bird that habitually holds its tail upright; noisy, busy animal; it builds large, bulky stick nests in tree holes or bird houses; found in developed areas, woodland clearings, etc.

**Common Nighthawk**
- drab, grayish-brown bird much like a Whip-poor-will (see page 27), with white bars across wings (when flying); largely nocturnal; often seen hawking for insects at dusk or heard overhead giving its distinctive *"peeent"* call.

**Catbird**
- sleek, charcoal-gray mockingbird with a black cap; named for its cat-like *"meahhh"* call note; sings a long series of separate musical notes; found commonly in low shrubbery, woodland edges and ravines.

## Brown Thrasher
- large, reddish-brown mockingbird with conspicuously black-speckled breast; sings like a Catbird (above), but repeats each note twice; found commonly in shrubby fields, woodland edges, etc.

## Yellow Warbler
- brilliant yellow, active and cheery little bird; commonly nests in open, isolated shrubs in overgrowing meadows and in upland thickets; a frequent victim of cowbird parasitism (see page ).

## Chestnut-sided Warbler
- small greenish bird with a yellow cap and narrow chestnut-coloured stripe along its side; nests in shrubbery at woodland edges and long overgrown pasturelands in sandy areas; song sounds like *"Pleased-pleased-pleased-to-meet-ya"* !

## American Redstart
- like a frantic, miniature oriole; often flashes the orange (male) or yellow (female) patches in its tail feathers when excited; common in shrubby woodland edges; migrates to Central America each winter.

**Chipping Sparrow**
-slim, brown (above) and gray (below) sparrow with a rufous cap and striking black and white eye line; sings a long, rapid trill; commonly found in dry, shrubby areas in meadows and woodland clearings.

**Vesper Sparrow**
- robust, pale brown, striped sparrow with chestnut shoulder patch and flashing white outer tail feathers; found in open, dry, sandy fields, gravel pits and along roadsides; an early spring migrant, rarely wintering.

**White-throated Sparrow**
- chunky, brownish bird with striking black and white head stripes and distinctive yellow spot before the eye; found in young, dry woodland edges and clearings; song described as saying "*Oh-sweet-Canada-Canada-Canada*"; a common migrant through backyards.

**Meadow Vole**
- an undistinguished, brownish lump of fur with a short tail; active year round and probably the Capital's most common mammal but infrequently seen because of nocturnal and subterranean habits; found in open, dry meadows and clearings.

**Red Fox**
- small, delicate, reddish-brown dog with slim features and a long bushy tail; typically found in shrubby meadows, old pastures and woodland edges; hunts mostly at night and preys largely on small birds and mammals.

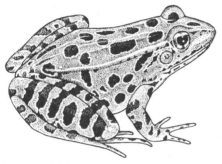

**Leopard Frog**
- medium-sized brown or usually green frog with rounded, blackish spots; breeds in wetlands but forages commonly in low meadows and tall-grass pastures for insects; its song is a low snore usually ending with a few rapid chuckles.

**Eastern Garter Snake**
- dark-bodied snake with three bright yellow stripes, one down the back and one on each side; commonly encountered in meadows and in shrubby areas, searching for frogs, worms and other small prey; hibernates in underground dens (hibernacula).

47

Farm & Country

**Rural village, Burritt's Rapids**
*(W.K. Gummer)*

Farming followed hard on the heels of the first loggers in the Capital and has been a common and vital industry here for almost 200 years. Not surprisingly, most of the land with reasonable to high potential for agriculture has been under continuous cultivation for more than a century. For the Capital area this has meant over a hundred years of ever-expanding open plains and meadows. This could only be achieved at the expense of the natural vegetation that preceded it. Most of the upland and small wetland areas of the Capital except for the Canadian Shield area have been converted to farmland of one kind or another.

Since great effort is made to ensure that only crop and livestock species of plants and animals prosper on farmland, the number of native species present is severely restricted. Ironically, it is because of the artificial nature of this situation that many troublesome weed species are able to survive; they don't have to respond to the checks and balances that are weighing on native associations.

There is a great degree of variation in the plants and animals found on different types of farmland. Short-grass crops, be they sod farms, pasture or golf courses, offer little for breeding native wildlife. These areas provide important resting and feeding grounds for migrating waterfowl, shorebirds and gulls, however. Some breeding species like the Starling, Coyote, Gray Partridge, Killdeer and Brown-headed Cowbirds also use these areas for feeding. All are either immigrants (the Coyote and Brown-headed Cowbird from the southwest, the Starling and Gray Partridge from Europe) or were less common natives that have increased their numbers tremendously in the Capital in the last century.

Grain crops such as corn, oats and wheat become alarmingly attractive to migrating seed eating birds like Red-winged Blackbirds, Common Grackles and Common Crows in the fall. After the fall harvest migrating geese - often in the thousands - rest on the stubble fields with other waterfowl and eat what spilled seed they can find amongst the furrows. They offer no threat to the agricultural use of the land.

Orchards are agricultural lands but they are also well organized, selectively established forests. Apple orchards, for example, are attractive to nesting birds such as flycatchers and orioles. These birds are drawn to the nesting sites provided by the trees themselves and by the abundant insect life associated with the flowers, fruit and leaves of the orchard. Starlings, American Robins and other fruit eating birds can conflict with the farmer. The fruit remaining on the trees can be an important source of food for winter visitors like Pine Grosbeaks, Bohemian Waxwings and Evening Grosbeaks. Even the occasional American Robin will winter in the Capital, usually depending on a continuing source of fruit for its survival. The plant life in orchards is primarily non-native.

The buildings and physical developments on the rural landscape offer many attractive opportunities for wildlife. Rock Doves, House Sparrows, Eastern Phoebes and Barn Swallows nest on such structures and feed near them. Spillage at feed lots , from feeding troughs and during seeding operations provide additional food for such species and for the many small mammals that search the night landscape. Hedges, wind breaks, shade trees and gardens also offer nesting sites, shelter and food for many animals.

It is probably in the Farm & Country habitats where man and nature are most in conflict in the Capital. The farmer works hard to obtain the greatest benefit possible from the land, using the skills and knowledge passed down by generations of his kin. Many plants and animals are also competing to get their greatest benefit from the same land, using the adaptive advantages passed down by generations of *their* kin. Pesticides, herbicides, guns, traps,and wetland drainage are amongst the tools used by the farmer to counter the persistence, sheer numbers and elusiveness of his wild competitors. This battle between man and nature is less pronounced in winter when the fields are left to Snowy Owls searching for Meadow Voles beneath the mantle of snow, to Gray Partridge scouring weed stalks for seeds and to Red Foxes searching for anything edible that they can dispatch. I quickly learned respect and admiration for those creatures that can endure - and even thrive - in winter farmlands.

## Some Places to Visit

**Central Experimental Farm**
- McCooey and Ash Lanes (migrating gulls and shorebirds in spring and fall; Snowy Owls and Gray Partridge in winter).
- Arboretum (wintering birds; migrating forest birds).
- Agricultural Museum area (flocks of resident House Sparrows and Rock Doves).

**The Burnt Lands**
- along Highway 44 and the County Line (open pasture lands).

**Green's Creek Conservation Area**
- west side of the creek (weedy croplands and pasture).

**Cobb's Lake**
- sides of Bear Brook road (resting waterfowl in migration).

**Quack Grass** *(Agropyron repens)*
- tall, coarse grass with narrow leaves and narrow, dense flowering spike arising singly from a long rhizome; a common pasture grass that is widely established in old pastures, along roadways and in disturbed areas.

**Foxtail Grass** *(Hordeum jubatum)*
- low, tufted grass with large, wispy spikelets; usually growing in large numbers in wet,disturbed pastures, about buildings and in wet (especially salty) ditches; originally from western North America but is now an increasingly common weed of agricultural areas in the Capital.

**Brome Grass** *(Bromus inermis)*
- tall, coarse grass with numerous slim, spreading or drooping spikelets; a common introduced pasture grass that has spread along roadways and throughout developed and agricultural areas.

**Lady's-thumb** *(Polygonum persicaria)*
- sprawling, dark green knotweed with long, often drooping pinkish-white flower clusters and small plain leaves; a dark "thumb print" mark is usually apparent on each leaf; a common weed (from Europe) in agricultural fields and disturbed areas.

**Tall Buttercup** *(Ranunculus acris)*
- a tall, dark green buttercup with broad, deeply dissected leaves and shiny yellow cup-shaped flowers; a European plant long established in wet agricultural fields, ditches and open ground; can be poisonous to the touch, or if eaten, for some people.

**Stinging Nettle** *(Urtica dioica)*
- tall, stringy, dark-green plant that grows in dense stands; tiny spines on leaves and stem contain a poison that results in a painful (but short lived) burning sensation when touched; usually found in moist ground.

**Bladder Campion** *(Silene vulgaris)*
- low, spreading plant with short, opposite leaves and flared, white and gray flowers with inflated bases; called 'poppers' by children for the loud 'pop' made when the flower is smacked between two hands; a European plant now found commonly in open, disturbed ground.

**Common Raspberry** *(Rubus strigosus)*
- tall, spreading bristly shrub with hairy leaves that are pale green below; usually found in large stands; white flowers bloom in late spring and develop into delicious red berries by mid summer in dry, sunny areas along fencelines, woodland edges, old roadways, etc.

**Alfalfa** *(Medicago sativa)*
- large, bright green bean with small, oblong leaves arranged in threes; flowers are complex, deep purple blooms; an important fodder and pasture plant that commonly becomes established along roadways, lanes, and disturbed sites .

**Evening Primrose** *(Oenothera parviflora)*
- a tall, many-flowered, pale green plant with numerous showy yellow flowers; found commonly in meadows, pastures and open ground; a native species (though grown as an ornamental in Europe); contains an oil which may aid in the treatment of multiple sclerosis.

**Blue Vetch** *(Vicia cracca)*
- low, straggling, vine-like bean with numerous small, narrow leaflets on each leaf and clusters of blue, bird-shaped flowers on separate branches; a European species now commonly established in meadows, pastures and croplands throughout the Capital.

**Wild Carrot** *(Daucus carota)*
- large, white, flat-topped flower clusters (each with a single, tiny purple flower in the center) is distinctive for this carrot; thought to be an ancestor of the domestic plant; a common introduction in old pastures, dry fields and roadsides.

**Lilac** *(Syringa vulgaris)*
- a tall, bushy shrub with smooth, pointed, dark green leaves and striking spikes of fragrant, blue or white flowers; widely persisting from ornamental plantings and frequently encountered at old farmstead sites.

**Morning Glory** *(Convolvulus sepium)*
- a trailing vine with large, arrowhead-shaped leaves and trumpet-shaped flowers; stem winds (always counter-clockwise) around other plants; both native and introduced forms occur here; found in croplands, along fencerows, at woodland edges and in open ground.

**Common Milkweed** *(Asclepias syriaca)*
- tall, coarse plant with thick, downy leaves, ball-like clusters of white and purple flowers and long, hairy seed pods; long known for a variety of human applications; milky juice produces natural rubber; fibers produce hemp; found in open areas.

**Butter-and-Eggs** *(Linaria vulgaris)*
- a low plant with narrow, dark green leaves and numerous showy, yellow and white flowers; a common European introduction that is found in open ground and agricultural areas across Canada; flowers in mid to late summer.

**Burdock** *(Arctium minus)*
- large, low, sprawling plant with huge, heart-shaped leaves; round, purple composite flowers borne on the ends of branches produce large, bristly burs which easily attach to clothes and fur; a European species now well established in dry, open sites in cropland.

**Mullein** *(Verbascum thapsus)*
- very tall, gray-green, downy plant with large leaves and a slender spike of showy yellow flowers; shape and texture of basal leaves earn the nickname "rabbit-ears"; a common European introduction into dry meadows, fields and roadsides.

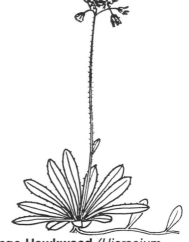

**Yarrow** *(Achillea millefolium)*
- a delicate plant with finely cut leaves and clusters of numerous, tiny white flowers; both introduced and (mostly) native forms occur here; found commonly in open, dry ground where it flowers throughout the summer; long considered to have herbal properties.

**Orange Hawkweed** *(Hieracium aurantiacum)*
- low perennial with a cluster of long, hairy leaves at ground level and numerous bright orange flowers atop a straight stem; in dry, sterile soil of roadsides, old pastures and woodland edges; common and still expanding its range.

**Brown-eyed Susan** *(Rudbeckia hirta)*
- tall plant with large, striking yellow flowers with dark centers; long, narrow, hairy leaves are clustered near the bottom of the stem; a European plant found commonly in open meadows, pastures and roadsides.

**Canada Goose**
- large, black-necked goose with distinctive white "chin" mark; migrates through the Capital in the tens of thousands; found in large flocks on flooded cropland in spring and in harvested grain fields in the fall; migrates at night.

**Mallard**
- bright green head, chestnut-coloured chest and brown body distinguish the male of this familiar water bird; the female is a plain brown colour and streaked; very common nester along weedy creek, ditch and pond banks; increasingly common winter resident.

**Snowy Owl**
- large, all-white owl (females and immatures are speckled with black); hunts during the day, mostly for mice and voles; a regular visitor in most winters; found in open, snow covered agricultural lands; nests in the high arctic.

**American Kestrel**
- a Blue Jay-sized falcon; males reddish-brown with blue wings and females dull brown and streaked; nests in old woodpecker holes in dead trees in old pastures and cropland areas; hunts in open areas for insects and small rodents.

**Upland Sandpiper**
- elegant but plainly coloured shorebird with yellow legs; often seen sitting alone on fenceposts or telephone poles by moist pasture and short-grass meadows; has a distinctive quivering wingbeat in flight.

**Gray Partridge**
- busy brown "butter-ball" with gray underparts and flashing orange tail; a permanent resident of open cropland and weedy fields; travels in large flocks in the winter; seldom seen in eastern Canada outside the Ottawa Valley.

**Killdeer**
- common, brazen and distinctive shorebird with two black bars across its white chest; loudly proclaims its name in its call; will perform an elaborate "broken-wing" act to lure intruders away from its nest; found in open areas.

**Black-bellied Plover**
- chunky shorebird with jet-black underparts and silvery upper parts in spring; somber grayish-white in fall; breeds in the arctic but migrates through the Capital, seen in small numbers along rivershores and uncommonly in large flocks in plowed fields.

**Horned Lark**
- a small, brown lark with yellow, white and black face markings; the first migrant each year, found singing its beautiful tinkling song from fence posts in open agricultural areas by mid February; nests on the ground.

**Mourning Dove**
- sleek, grayish-brown with a long, white-margined, pointed tail; mournful *"Whoo-wooho-woe-woe-woe"* song gives it its name; common breeder and increasingly frequent wintering species at bird feeders.

**Barn Swallow**
- exotic looking blue swallow with red-brown face, pale underparts and long, deeply forked tail; sweeps across open pastures at break-neck speed a few centimetres above the ground in pursuit of flying insects; nests on bridges and buildings .

## Brown-headed Cowbird
- small, sleek blackbird; males are black with brown head and females are uniformly gray; a prairie bird that followed Bison herds to catch the insects these cattle stirred up; now follows livestock; leaves its eggs in other birds' nests and moves on.

## Eastern Kingbird
- aggressive, noisy, black and white flycatcher that perches conspicuously on fencelines, telephone wires and treetops; found in pastures and croplands as well as wetland areas; earns its scientific name *Tyrannus* by fearless defence of its young.

## Eastern Meadowlark
- beautiful pale brown bird with bright yellow breast marked with a bold black V; a common species of open pastures and meadows; an early migrant, announcing the season by its song that sounds like *"Spring-of-the-year"*.

## Savannah Sparrow
- small, brown-streaked sparrow with a distinctive yellow spot before its eye; common on wires of pasture fences or singing from weed tops; an insect-eating bird that migrates south in the fall.

**Snow Bunting**
- a slender finch with subdued brownish markings on its white body in winter; received the nickname "snowflake" from its black and white flashing wings and twinkling flight pattern; winters here, sometimes in large numbers; breeds in the arctic.

**Woodchuck**
- large, chunky, brown marmot; found commonly in meadows, pastures and along roadway margins where the soil is deep enough for its burrows; feeds on green vegetable material, including clover and alfalfa; hibernates underground in the winter.

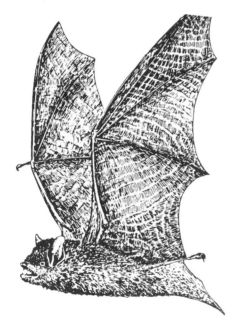

**Little Brown Bat**
- small, uniformly brown flying mammal; commonly found hunting for flying insects at night over fields, clearings and waterbodies; uses a form of sonar to echo-locate its prey; hibernates through the winter in large groups.

**Coyote**
- a small, reddish-brown wolf with a thin, fox-like muzzle; usually carries its tail low when running; found in croplands, scrubby woodland edges and fields in small family groups; feeds on small mammals (especially voles) and birds.

**American Toad**
- squat, brown, reddish-brown or gray amphibian with numerous bumps on its skin; hops (frogs jump); sings a long, high, insect-like trill; forages in croplands and gardens for insects, worms and other invertebrates.

Urban Landscape

**Urban bird feeder**
*(John Major, The Ottawa Citizen)*

# URBAN LANDSCAPE

Although the development of buildings, roadways and houses generally has meant the destruction of the natural vegetation as it had existed for centuries in Canada's Capital, we are not without plant and animal life in our cities. Many non-native species thrive in the artificial conditions created by the urban and suburban landscape, as do a surprising number of native species.

The nature of the shelters we build for our own protection - houses, apartment buildings, offices - encourages use by various wildlife species. Our consumer society produces an abundance of waste which is used to help form nests and shelters for many animals and offers food for others. The nooks and crannies of roof eaves, window ledges and basement corners provide cover and protection. The value of this protection is particularly evident in winter. Rows of Starlings and House Sparrows huddled on the hot air outlets of chimneys or along south-facing window ledges indicate one way in which we inadvertently aid these creatures. The rapid rise in population of scavenging birds like Ring-billed Gulls and Starlings is significantly affected by the spread of fast-food restaurants with outdoor garbage bins.

Throughout the Capital, backyard winter bird feeders are a frequent and cheery sight. It really is amazing how many individual birds can be sustained by one feeder. Starlings, House Sparrows and Rock Doves certainly take advantage of this bounty, as do thousands of native birds. A horde of Evening Grosbeaks (knowingly called "greedies" by many feeder owners !), Black-capped Chickadees, Blue Jays, White-breasted Nuthatches and even the uncommon and spectacular Cardinal, can combine to clean out a feeder in no time. They pay their benefactors back in full, however, by providing a winter-long spectacle of colour, sound and action.

The Urban Landscape can successfully replicate natural conditions for some species. The endangered Peregrine Falcon is a spectacular example. Reintroduction efforts have focused on establishing office towers in the Capital as home base for released young falcons. These serve as artificial versions of the huge cliffs on which they normally would be fledged. It is hoped that one day some of these magnificent hawks will breed on one of the "urban cliffs" here in the Capital. Similarly, if somewhat less spectacularly, the Chimney Swift that once nested in hollow trees and rock crevices has adapted to the urban equivalent offered by office building chimneys. Although probably most common in the days when all buildings were heated by wood or coal and required large chimneys, the swift is still more common today than it would have been when the Capital was covered in forests. An even more total commitment to man-made habitat is demonstrated by the Purple Martin, a large colonial swallow that has completely forsaken its natural nesting sites. I am not aware of any records of martins nesting in the Capital in other than man-made structures, nor have I witnessed this anywhere in the species' range. Nestboxes, by the way, are a very good means of encouraging wild birds to live and breed in urban areas.

Roadways provide valuable habitat for many plants and animals, some with very particular requirements. Salt-tolerant plants, for example, have become well established in ditches where years of winter de-icing programs have inadvertently supplied an ample salt supply. Woodchucks are common and

67

have grown fat on the clover-covered side slopes of the Queensway and other major highways in the Capital. Red-winged Blackbirds have spread up from the marshes into backyard cedar hedges and Lilac bushes to nest - a most striking event in the last two decades in the city.

The constant competition for food, shelter and breeding sites seems more open to observation in the Urban Landscape than in the wild; this is most instructive of what goes on in the natural world, if at a slower pace.

## Some Places to Visit

- any urban area throughout the Capital, especially where shelter and food may be available.
- winter bird feeders maintained by the Ottawa Field Naturalists at:

- Pink Road, Aylmer (with Club des ornithologues de l'Outaouais (Hull) personnel).

- Jack Pine Trail, Stony Swamp Conservation Area.

- Rockcliffe Park.

- Pine Grove Trail, Gloucester.

These feeders are operated in winter only.

**Salt-meadow Grass** *(Puccinellia distans)*
- like a squat Kentucky Blue Grass (above) but stiffly branched; grows in dense, pure stands in salty, wet ditches along major highways; now abundant though only first found here in 1969; a European plant originally.

**Witch Grass** *(Panicum capillare)*
- a low, much branched, densely hairy grass; a native annual; flowering heads break off and roll in the wind, spreading the seed; formerly restricted to river floodplains but now abundant in backyards, along roads and open areas.

**Crab Grass** *(Digitaria ischaemum)*
- a low, coarse, purple-green grass with narrow leaves and long, thin fruiting heads atop bare branching stems; a common weed of European origin in lawns, along roadsides and in gardens.

**Mouse-ear Chickweed** *(Cerastium fontanum)*
- low, branched, gray-green little plant with hairy leaves and stem; small white flowers with deeply notched petals; blooms through the summer; a common weed of European origin in lawns, gardens and open sites.

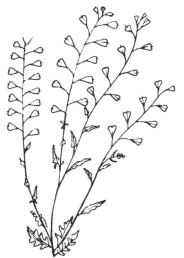

**Shepherd's-purse** *(Capsella bursa-pastoris)*
- small, dark green mustard with deeply cut leaves, white flowers and triangular seedpods (shaped like a shepherd's purse of long ago); a European plant now common in lawns, gardens and disturbed sites in the Capital.

**Silvery Cinquefoil** *(Potentilla argentea)*
- low, sprawling little plant with deeply incised leaves that are dark green above and silvery below; small yellow flowers bloom most of the summer; a common weed of European origin in open rocky ground, walkways and roadsides.

**Pepper-grass** *(Lepidium densiflorum)*
- small, dark green mustard with dense spikes of flat, oval seedpods; a common introduced weed of disturbed ground, in pavement crevices, along roadsides and other open sites; said to have various herbal properties.

**Birds-foot Trefoil** *(Lotus corniculatus)*
- sprawling, bright green clover-like bean with conspicuous yellow flowers; has spread from planting as a cover plant along roadsides; common along highways and in weedy fields throughout the Capital.

70

**Viper's-bugloss** *(Echium vulgare)*
- erect, bristly blackish-green plant with many bright blue flowers and reddish flower buds; a common weed of open, dry, rocky ground of roadsides, pathways and other disturbed sites, usually in large stands.

**White Sweet-clover** *(Melilotus alba)*
- tall, much branched pale green bean with numerous small white flowers; a common weed of European origin along roadways, railway tracks and dry, open areas; the seeds are a favoured food of migrating sparrows in the fall.

**Yellow Wood-sorrel** *(Oxalis fontana)*
- tiny, sprawling shamrock-like plant with pale yellow flowers held aloft on separate stalks; commonly found as a weed in gardens, in cracks in sidewalks and other disturbed sites.

**Deadly Nightshade** *(Solanum dulcamara)*
- trailing, vine-like, shrubby plant with deeply lobed leaves, purple flowers with yellow centers and bright red berries; an introduced relative of the tomato found in dry, rocky disturbed ground; of European origin.

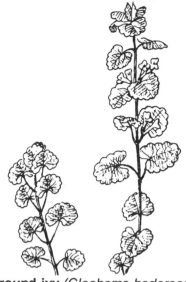

**Ground-ivy** *(Glechoma hederacea)*
- small, creeping, dark green plant with round, wavy-edged leaves and complex blue flowers; forms large mats, excluding other plants, in sandy lawns and grassy areas.

**Common Plantain** *(Plantago major)*
- low, dark green little plant with sprawling, oblong leaves and narrow heads of greenish flowers projecting above them; common in lawns, along walkways and by roadsides.

**Common Speedwell** *(Veronica officinale)*
- small, coarse, creeping plant with oval, hairy leaves and spikes of small, blue flowers; a common weed of European origin in gardens, lawns and open, disturbed ground.

**Ragweed** *(Ambrosia artemisiifolia)*
- small, dark green plant with deeply cut leaves and spikes of tiny, lamp-like flowers; pollen is produced abundantly in late summer and is *the* prime offender for hay fever sufferers; found in open, disturbed ground.

**Dandelion** *(Taraxacum officinale)*
- low, yellow-flowered composite with deeply cut, reflexed leaves; seed heads form downy balls with each seed held beneath a wispy "umbrella" for wind transport; a familiar European weed of lawns, roadsides and other open sites.

**Peregrine Falcon**
- crow-sized hawk with black "teardrop" mark below the eye; adults are blue-gray above, immatures are brown and streaked; an endangered species being reintroduced at nest sites on buildings in Ottawa and Hull; preys on birds.

**Pineapple-weed** *(Matricaria matricarioides)*
- small, light green plant with finely cut leaves and small white flowers with yellow centers; crushed leaves smell strongly of pineapple; a common weed of European origin in lawns, trampled paths and other disturbed sites.

**Rock Dove**
- large, chunky dove of various colours but always with a blunt, square tail; actually feral pigeons brought from Europe; a permanent resident now, nesting on buildings and in quarries; feeds mostly on seeds but also human food scraps.

## Chimney Swift
- looks like a "cigar on wings"; flies with a rapid, twinkling wing beat and constant twittering; formerly nested in hollow trees but adapted well to chimney walls; less common since the establishment of central heating.

## Cliff Swallow
- striking blue swallow with orange face and rump patches; squared tail; builds elaborate gourd-shaped nests of mud under roof eaves and bridges, usually by rivers; several large colonies are known along the Ottawa River.

## American Robin
- robust thrush with a dark back and brick-red breast; a familiar bird of backyards, city parks and gardens; feeds on worms and other invertebrates as well as fruit; will nest on houses and also in trees; most migrate south in the fall.

## Common Starling
- squat, noisy black bird; speckled white in winter and iridescent black in summer; common in backyards, at fast food restaurants and dumps - wherever food might be found; a European species first seen in the Capital about 1920.

**House Sparrow**
- perky, brown and white finch (not truly a sparrow); males with a black "bib" and females dull gray-brown; a European bird introduced into North America in the 19th century; now abundant in urban areas north to the arctic.

**Gray Squirrel**
- robust, black or gray squirrel with pale underparts and a large, bushy tail; black form is most common in the Capital (gray is more common to the south); a resident of city parks, back yards and treed areas.

**Norway Rat**
- large gray rodent with a long, bare tail; a European animal now found in buildings and other urban structures where it forages (at night) for any plant or animal foods; a carrier of disease and a serious sanitation problem.

**House Finch**
- small, chunky, brown finch; males with red face and chest patches, females streaked; an introduction that frequents bird feeders; first noticed in Ontario in the early 1970's; now a regularly seen resident in the Capital.

**House Mouse**
- small, large-eared rodent with a long, bare tail; a European introduction (likely from the British Isles) now common in buildings and farms; a serious crop pest and sanitation problem.

**Striped Skunk**
- a chunky, black and white striped weasel with a large bushy tail and waddling gait; frequently found in suburban back yards and city parks; nocturnal hunter of frogs and small mammals as well as feeding on human garbage.

**Forested Wetland**

**Silver Maple Swamp, Kanata**
*(D.F. Brunton)*

# FORESTED WETLANDS

From an airplane, Forested Wetlands look very much like Upland Forest - a mixture of stands of trees of about the same age and dimension. The critical difference is obvious only from ground level; it is wet here. This permanent or prolonged flooding eliminates the many plants and animals that are unsuited to the wetness and shade of these swamp lands. As a consequence, some of the Capital's more unusual species are found in this habitat.

Forested Wetlands are common along the shores and on islands of major rivers in the Capital, especially the Ottawa and Rideau Rivers. The extensive spring flooding that follows ice break-up serves to provide fresh water to swamps cut off from the rivers for the remainder of the year. It enriches the soil with new layers of sediment and cleans off ground debris left from the previous year. The Silver Maple - Red Maple swamp is an attractive example of this rivershore habitat. The slow and irregular growth of trees in such sites has discouraged commercial logging and the intermittent flooding restricts development. Thus, some of the oldest forests in Canada's Capital are Silver and Red Maple swamps. Vast beds of Ostrich Fern develop under such cover on the low, wet islands in the Ottawa River downstream from the cities of Ottawa and Hull.

Another widespread example of Forested Wetland results not from its location by a waterway so much as from the actions of an animal. Beavers dam creeks to create ponds, flooding the adjacent forest and forming swamps of dead and dying trees. This constitutes excellent breeding habitat for a variety of birds, including Tree Swallow, several species of woodpecker and the spectacular Wood Duck. These small Forested Wetlands are found throughout the Capital's Upland Forest areas, creating islands of wetland habitat that quickly develop into marsh or wet meadow (see Open Wetlands).

Away from the rivers, a variety of hardwood species (including Black and Green Ash, Red Maple and White Elm) occupy non-acidic sites. This mixed Forest Wetland is slowly transformed into a swamp forest dominated by Red Maple, often with scattered clumps of White Cedar or even Eastern Hemlock within it. This maple forest casts heavy shade upon the sea of Ostrich and Cinnamon Fern - and little else - that covers the forest floor. At the margins of such swamps where the ground slopes down from the Upland Forest, wetland vegetation mixes with and eventually gives way to species of drier ground.

In a relatively few localities across the Capital wet areas with poor drainage have developed deep, permanently saturated, acidic, organic deposits of dead and living moss. Here, a distinctive type of coniferous Forested Wetland occurs, dominated by Black Spruce, Tamarack and White Cedar. These bog forests as they are known, are few in number but large in extent in the Capital. The Mer Bleue Conservation Area in Gloucester contains a large portion of one of the most extensive bogs in southern Ontario. Across the Canadian Shield on the Quebec side of the Ottawa River, however, the acidic nature of the ground has helped to encourage the development of many smaller bog forests in sites that are constantly wet and cool. These habitats are found across northern Canada. Consequently, species normally found far to the north of the Capital can be moderately common in this habitat.

While hardwood Forested Wetlands may support many of the same canopy birds as those in Upland Forest, bog forests have a distinctively different bird life. Even the common species show an affinity to those in areas of northern Ontario and Quebec. This is demonstrated by the plant life of bog forests as well.

# Some Places to Visit

**Gatineau Park**
- Champlain Lookout Trails (swamp forest of beaver ponds).
- Ramsay Lake (bog forest along lake margin).

**Leamy Lake Park**
- mouth of Leamy Creek (ancient Silver Maple swamp forest).
- Ottawa/Gatineau River shores and Leamy Creek (ash-elm swamps).

**McLaurin Bay**
- along peninsula by rivershore (old Silver Maple swamp forest).

**Marlborough Forest**
- Roger Stevens Road near Rideau Trail (Black Ash-White Elm swamps).
- Rideau Trail near Flood Road alvar (White Cedar swamps).

**Stony Swamp Conservation Area**
- Trail 5, Richmond Road (by powerline) (White Cedar and Black Ash swamps).
- Jack Pine Trail (White Cedar swamp and beaver pond swamps).

**Stillwater Creek**
- along recreational pathway (old maple-elm bottomland forest with Black Maple).

**Britannia Conservation Area**
- east of filtration plant (young, rich Silver Maple swamp and Green Ash shore forest).
- south end of Mud Lake (maple-willow swamp).

**Pinhey Forest Reserve**
- north of Slack Road (mature Red Maple swamp).
- south of Slack Road (Silver Maple - White Cedar swamp forest).

**Baxter Conservation Area**
- along self-guiding trail (mature Red-Silver Maple swamp forest).

**Mer Bleue Conservation Area**
- boardwalk trail off Borthwick Ridge (Black Spruce forest).
- distant view from Borthwick and Dolman Ridges (Black Spruce-Larch bog forests).

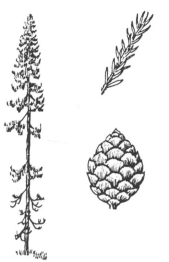

**Cinnamon Fern** *(Osmunda cinnamomea)*
- tall, broad-leaved, pale green fern growing in robust clumps; spore bodies are on a dark brown modified leaf in the center of the clump; found commonly and often as a dominant in sandy, wet ground in hardwood swamps.

**Black Spruce** *(Picea mariana)*
- thin, spindly spruce with short needles and slightly hairy twigs; a dominant tree on wet, organic peat in bogs across Canada and locally distributed in the Capital (e.g. the Mer Bleue bog, see page 171).

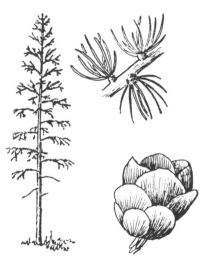

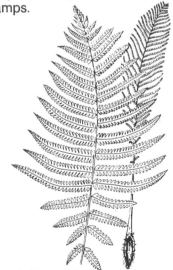

**Tamarack** *(Larix laricina)*
- thin, much branched larch tree with delicate, pale green needles and numerous cones: found in open, wet (especially calcareous) meadows and peat mats; the only conifer in the Capital that loses its needles in the fall.

**Ostrich Fern** *(Matteuccia struthiopteris)*
- tall, dark green, broad-leaved fern; grows in large tufts with plume-like central leaf containing the spore bodies; forms huge stands in rivershore maple and elm swamps; the "fiddlehead" fern of the Maritimes.

**Eastern White Cedar** *(Thuja occidentalis)*
- densely-branched conifer with tiny, flat, scale-like leaves and numerous small cones at the end of branches; found commonly in pure or mixed stands in wet, mossy sites (especially calcareous areas) in the Capital.

**Clearweed** *(Pilea pumila)*
- a delicate, pale-green plant with translucent leaves and tiny greenish-white flowers; found commonly in hardwood swamps and shoreline forests across the Capital, often growing in deep shade.

**Jack-in-the-Pulpit** *(Arisaema triphyllum)*
- dark green, three-leaved plant with a peculiar flowering structure known as a spathe (the *pulpit*); the flowers are held on a column inside known as the spadix (*Jack*); common in wet shady ground throughout the Capital.

**Skunk Current** *(Ribes glandulosum)*
- low, sprawling shrub with maple leaf-shaped leaves and clusters of plump, bristly berries on ascending branches; common in wet, sandy or boggy ground in hardwood and mixed swamps; twigs and leaves have a strong skunk-like odour.

**Black Ash** *(Fraxinus nigra)*
- tall, straight-trunked tree with deeply ridged, gray bark and large compound leaves with pale green, drooping leaflets; a member of the olive family; common in wet sandy sites (especially acidic ones) with elm, cedar and fir.

**Silver Maple** *(Acer saccharinum)*
- large, many-branched tree with deeply cut leaves; forms large stands in wet, sandy rivershore swamps and on islands; frequently planted as an ornamental along city streets.

**Silky Dogwood** *(Cornus amomum ssp. obliqua)*
- tall, many-branched bush with gray branches and narrow, pale green leaves that turn coppery coloured in the fall; clusters of bluish-white berries develop on branch tips; a southern species that is common in the Capital along major rivers.

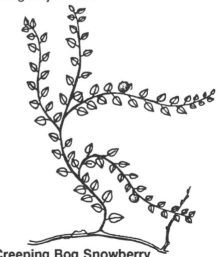

**Creeping Bog Snowberry** *(Gaultheria hispidula)*
- tiny, prostrate vine-like heath with dark green leaves; large white berries develop singly amongst the leaves; in cool, moist, acidic conifer woods on moss and peat in the Gatineau Hills and rarely in Ottawa-Carleton.

**Swamp Loosestrife** *(Lysimachia ciliata)*
- tall, branched plant with tapering, pale green leaves and drooping cup-shaped flowers with distinctively fringed yellow petals; found in wet, calcareous shaded sites in hardwood swamps and thickets.

**Nodding Beggarticks** *(Bidens cernua)*
- variably shaped dark green plant with conspicuous yellow flowers and long, narrow, uncut leaves; seeds form tiny "pitchforks" that catch in fur or on socks and pants in the fall; in wet, shaded or open sites.

**Green-backed Heron**
- dark, crow sized heron with iridescent bluish-green back and reddish-brown striped neck; often first noticed by its explosive *"keow"* call note as it flies off; inconspicuous day-feeding "skulker" in thickets and swamps.

84

## Wood Duck

- spectacular harlequin pattern of the male is unmistakable; female is plainer; normally a shy duck, often heard (a plaintive "oo-eehh" note) as it flushes before being seen; nests in holes high in trees in swamps adjacent to open water.

## Tree Swallow

- perky swallow with shiny blue-green back; females with duller (almost brown) colours; returns in early April and nests in tree holes in swamps; forms huge post-breeding roosts (e.g. at Pembroke, Ontario) in the late summer.

## Brown Creeper

-small, brown-striped bird that hops *up* tree trunks searching for insects in bark crevices; a resident in coniferous swamps (and upland forests); known by its high, thin *"zeeeet"* call note and beautiful spring song.

## Golden-crowned Kinglet
- tiny greenish blur of a bird with a conspicuous striped crown; never stops moving; nests uncommonly in coniferous swamps in the Gatineau Hills but a common migrant in the Capital; thin, quick "*zee-zee-zee*" call is distinctive.

## Black and White Warbler
- quick black and white striped bird that creeps nuthatch-like along tree trunks and limbs; feeds on insects; found commonly in coniferous and mixed forests such as cedar swamps in the Gatineau Hills.

## Warbling Vireo
- small, nondescript greenish-brown bird with a pale line through the eye; named for its long, warbling song; nests high in rivershore hardwoods and forages for insects in the canopy.

## Yellow-rumped Warbler (formerly Myrtle Warbler)
- beautiful, bouncy blue-gray bird with bright yellow rump and shoulder flashes and black striped underparts; uncommon breeder in coniferous bog forests in the Capital; very common migrant in spring and fall.

## Northern Waterthrush
- drab brown warbler with striped underparts; one of the few warblers that walks (flipping leaves, etc. in search of food); nests along creeks on upturned stumps and banks in hardwood or mixed swamp forests.

## Swamp Sparrow
- grayish-brown sparrow with reddish-brown cap; found in swamp thickets and young swamp forests; sings a simple trill (like a Chipping Sparrow); migrates to the south each winter.

## Common Grackle
- large, cocky blackbird with a long, broad tail, iridescent greenish-blue head and bright yellow eye; occurs widely, but nests commonly in swamp thickets and swamps as well as in urban areas; migrates in large flocks.

## Star-nosed Mole
- plain, gray-black lump of fur with short, muscular limbs, large feet and a bizarre, pink, feeler-tipped nose; mostly subterranean, burrowing for worms and other invertebrates as well as swimming for prey; found in swamp forests with loose soil.

**Blanding's Turtle**
- a high-domed, smooth-shelled, dark turtle with a characteristic bright yellow throat; found sunning on logs in hardwood swamps in Ottawa-Carleton.

**Raccoon**
- chunky, grayish carnivore with a distinctive black facial mask, bushy, ringed tail and long toes; forages at night for various aquatic animals as well as plant material in swamp forests and upland areas; active mostly in summer.

**Blue-spotted Salamander**
- long, blackish amphibian with numerous blue or bluish-white spots on the sides and belly; spends most of its time under logs, leaf litter, etc.; locally common, especially in hardwood swamp forests in spring.

**Open Wetland**

**Bog mat and aquatic plants, Masham**
*(P. Hall)*

# OPEN WETLANDS

In shallow depressions along waterways, in Upland Forest clearings and even in developed areas permanently wet, unforested sites are frequently encountered. These encompass a wide variety of habitats including sedge and grass meadows, marshes, alder thickets and open bog mats. They are often short lived stages in the regeneration of disturbed areas. Despite their regular occurrence, however, Open Wetlands have become less common as site after site has been filled in or drained. Over 70% of all wetlands in eastern Ontario have already been destroyed. This seriously reduces the landscape's ability to act as a reservoir. Under natural conditions these wetlands help to regulate run-off during peak melt and precipitation periods, act as filters to remove environmental pollutants from the water flow and support directly and indirectly a vast and intricate web of life.

In boggy areas where slowly developing bog forests have not yet filled in or in peatlands just recovering from a natural disturbance such as fire, open heath or sedge covered bog mats are established. Some of these are actually floating on a great depth of cold, inky-black, highly acidic water and quake when someone walks across them. On this fragile mat a unique set of plants and animals prospers. It includes species typical of the vast peatlands of northern Canada, as well as plants that actually eat insects in this nutrient-poor habitat.

Speckled Alder and willow thickets (or swales) occupy wet, fresh sites at locations where Forested Wetlands have not yet developed. Although the number of species in such habitats is small they are present in abundance. Anyone attempting to walk through a dense thicket of Speckled Alder, Red-osier Dogwood or willows will learn new respect for the term "bush-whacking"! Such vegetation is frequently found in old beaver ponds that have partially dried up or have become overgrown.

Perhaps the most familiar example of Open Wetland habitat is the cat-tail marsh (often erroneously called "bull-rushes"). A marsh is an area of shallow water which is dominated by standing vegetation that is anchored to the bottom. The cat-tail *(Typha)* marsh is found in areas recently disturbed (by flooding for example). It is an unusually productive system, supporting vast numbers of plants and animals including such familiar creatures as Painted Turtle, Bullfrog, Red-winged Blackbird and American Bittern. Through mechanical impact, burning, feeding by Muskrats or other factors, natural marshes are able periodically to renew themselves. Ironically, protecting marshes from the physical impact of natural disturbances has a negative effect. Without disturbance, the marsh becomes a solid, impenetrable cat-tail growth and, ultimately, Forested Wetland. Like so many other natural communities, marshes need the natural forces that shaped them - including the apparently destructive ones - to continue.

# Some Places to Visit

## Gatineau Park
- Ramsay Lake (marginal bog mat on lake and alder-willow swales).
- Champlain Lookout trails (overgrowing beaver meadows).
- Fortune Lake (old, extensive beaver meadow).

## McLaurin Bay
- margins of the lake (extensive cat-tail marsh).

## Marlborough Forest
- Richmond Fen (open fen meadows).
- along Roger Stevens Road ( cat-tail-willow marshes).

## Stony Swamp Conservation Area
- Richmond Road south of powerline (old cat-tail stand).
- Moodie Drive south of Jack Pine Trail ( cat-tail-loosestrife marsh).
- Moodie Drive at Knoxdale Road ( large alder-willow swale).

## Britannia Conservation Area
- south end of Mud Lake ( large Buttonbush swamp).
- edge of Mud Lake (dogwood-willow thickets).

## Andrew Haydon Park
- Ottawa Beach (Loosestrife-bullrush marsh and emergent shoreline).

## Baxter Conservation Area
- along trail (Speckled Alder thickets in clay soil).
- south end of trail (cat-tail marsh).

## Lower Duck Island
- east end of island (Buttonbush-dogwood thickets and grassy meadows).

## Mer Bleue Conservation Area
- edge of ridges (extensive Speckled Alder thickets and boggy cat-tail marsh).
- end of Borthwick Ridge (boardwalk trail on bog heath mat).

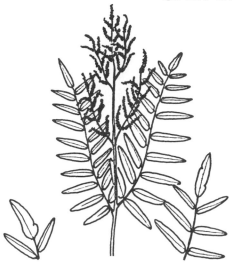

**Royal Fern** *(Osmunda regalis)*
- a tall, pale green fern with large, much divided leaves; spore bodies contained in modified upper portion of the leaves; found in wet, sandy or boggy ground in the open, especially in the Gatineau Hills.

**Canary-grass** *(Phalaris arundinacea)*
- tall grass with wide, long, dark green leaves and squat, robust flowering heads; introduced as a pasture grass and now widely distributed in wet meadows across the Capital; often forms dense stands.

**Canada Bluejoint** *(Calamagrostis canadensis)*
- tall, long leaved grass with large, many flowered, delicate flower heads; grows in extensive, pure stands on creek banks and low, wet meadows; an important source of natural fodder ('beaver hay') in pioneer days.

**Strong Bulrush** *(Scirpus validus)*
- a tall simple sedge that is topped by a number of plump seedheads on individual stalks; grows in open, shallow water at the edge of cat-tail marshes, often in extensive stands; not to be confused with cat-tail *(Typha)*.

93

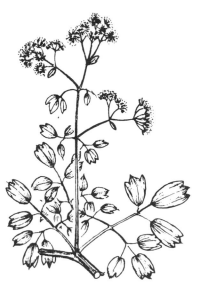

**Pitcher-plant** *(Sarracenia purpurea)*
- low, reddish-green plant with hollow, inflated leaves that hold water and a single, large, drooping flower on a central stalk; found in open bog mats; leaves trap insects which drown and are digested for nutrients.

**Meadow-rue** *(Thalictrum pubescens)*
- tall, sprawling, delicate buttercup with numerous small,tulip-shaped leaves; tiny white flowers are in clusters at the ends of branches; grows along river and pond shores and in wet meadows across the Capital.

**Round-leaved Sundew** *(Drosera rotundifolia)*
- tiny plant with round, reddish, long-stalked leaves covered by sticky droplets; small white flowers are held on a separate stalk above the leaves; found in wet, acidic ground of bog mats, wet gravel and sand; leaves trap insects as a source of nutrients.

**Steeplebush** *(Spiraea tomentosa)*
- steeple-shaped shrub with small, dark green leaves that are pale below; has a dense spike of pinkish-purple flowers at branch ends; a striking rose of wet, acidic shrubby areas and bog margins, especially in the Gatineau Hills.

**Touch-Me-Not** *(Impatiens capensis)*
- sprawling, delicate, pale green plant with spectacular orange flowers; seed capsules explode when touched to disperse the seed - hence its common name; found in wet ground of swamp and marsh edges and low meadows throughout the Capital.

**Northern Willowherb** *(Epilobium ciliatum)*
- a tall, narrow plant with long, narrow stem leaves and tiny pinkish-white flowers on short stems; fruit capsules are long and thin , containing many tiny seeds and a mass of downy fluff; common in wet meadows and thickets.

**Blue Violet** *(Viola cucullata)*
- low, tufted, bright green plant with broad, heart-shaped leaves and deep blue flowers arising singly on separate stalks; in wet shaded thickets, stream banks, etc.; flowering early in the spring.

**Purple Loosestrife** *(Lythrum salicaria)*
- tall, shrubby plant with a distinctive spike of many small, showy, purple flowers; abundant along open rivershore and in low meadows, especially in Ottawa-Carleton; a recently arrived European introduction that is seriously affecting native flora.

**Bulblet Water-hemlock** *(Cicuta bulbifera)*
- a delicate, much branched carrot with small leaves and open clusters of tiny white flowers; bulblets form along the stem and can propagate new plants when they drop off; common in wet, usually acidic ground of bog edges and meadows.

**Leatherleaf** *(Chamaedaphne calyculata)*
- wiry, dark-leaved shrub forming dense stands; sprays of small, bell-like white flowers droop from branches in early summer; found abundantly along boggy lake shores and on open peat mats, especially in the Gatineau Hills.

**Red-osier Dogwood** *(Cornus stolonifera)*
- sprawling, thicket-forming shrub with bright red branches; clusters of white flowers and (later) white berries form at branch ends; common in wet meadows, along shorelines and in low thickets.

**Bog Laurel** *(Kalmia polifolia)*
- low shrub with shiny, evergreen leaves and clusters of bright pink, upward facing blossoms; flowers in early June; found in open peat mats in the Gatineau Hills and rarely in Ottawa.

**Bog Cranberry** *(Vaccinium oxycoccus)*
- tiny, prostrate, vine-like heath with "shooting star"-like flowers drooping from stalks at the ends of branches; bright red berries develop in late summer; found abundantly but locally in open, wet, cool bog mats.

**Swamp Milkweed** *(Asclepias incarnata)*
- tall, smooth, seldom branched plant with long leaves and dull pink flowers in clusters; reddish-green seed pods develop in late summer; found in small numbers in wet meadows, marshes and rivershore thickets.

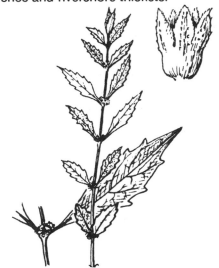

**Swamp-candles** *(Lysimachia terrestris)*
- a narrow spike of conspicuous yellow flowers is held atop an erect stem with few branches; leaves are tapered and light green; a primrose found commonly along wet rivershores, meadows and marsh edges.

**Northern Bugleweed** *(Lycopus uniflorus)*
- low, stiffly erect mint with small, jagged edged dark green leaves arising in pairs along the stem; flowers form clusters at leaf-stem junctions; found along wet shorelines, meadows and in wet thickets.

**Wild Mint** *(Mentha arvensis)*
. low, pale green, hairy plant with strong minty odour; clusters of tiny blue flowers are situated along the stem where leaves join it; common in wet meadows, grassy rivershores and pond margins.

**Nannyberry** *(Viburnum lentago)*
- tall, thicket forming shrub with leathery, tapered leaves that have finely serrated edges; large clusters of blackish, foul-smelling berries develop at branch ends in late summer; common along wet rivershores and low thickets.

**Blue Vervain** *(Verbena hastata)*
- tall, stiff plant with ragged, dark green leaves topped with spikes of tiny, bright blue flowers; common in open wet meadows, grassy rivershores and low thickets.

**Pied-billed Grebe**
-small, drab diving bird with a stubby black-marked bill; sings a long series of *cowh* notes from ponds in cat-tail marshes and weedy bays; nests on floating platforms in the marsh;can be seen swimming with brightly-striped young on its back.

**Black Duck**
- large, plain, blackish-brown dabbling duck with contrasting white underwings; nests along rivershores and marshes; migrates through the Capital in large numbers; some winter here; being reduced by competition from Mallards.

**Great Blue Heron**
- tall, stately, gray-blue heron (*not* a crane) with long legs and bill and distinctive head plumes;feeds on small animals (amphibians and fish - even mammals) in wet meadows, marshes and along rivershores; nests in colonies in trees.

**Blue-winged Teal**
- small dabbling duck; male with a striking white crescent on a blue head; female is plain brown (like a tiny mallard); large blue wing patches evident in flight; nests in marshes and in grassy areas adjacent ponds and rivers.

**Northern Harrier (formerly Marsh Hawk)**
- long winged, long tailed gray (male) or brown (female) raptor with slow, floppy flight; flies low over fields in search of small animals, dropping down onto the prey; nests on the ground in tall grass of low meadows or marshes.

### Short-eared Owl
- long winged, pale brown owl with moth-like flight; hunts like a harrier (see above) at dusk and dawn over marshes and wet meadows; uncommon and local raptor in the Capital, nesting on the ground in loose colonies.

### Common Snipe
- large, long-billed, brown-striped shorebird; found in wet meadows and cat-tail marshes; probes for invertebrates with its long bill; spectacular aerial display performed by the male in spring, including production of a winnowing sound from its tail feathers.

### Black Tern
- elegant, thin winged black tern called "sea-swallow" in some areas; seemingly in constant, noisy flight across cat-tail marshes; nests on Muskrat houses or floating platforms and feeds on small fish; migrates south each fall.

### Alder Flycatcher
- drab, greenish, inconspicuous little flycatcher with white eye-ring and wing-bars; found in alder thickets and wet, shrubby marsh edges; best (and often only) identified by its distinctive *Whee-bee-oo* call.

**Marsh Wren**
- active, noisy, little brown bird with striking white eyebrow line; chatters constantly while foraging for insects amongst cat-tails; nest is a ball of grass with a side entrance, built by the male in a clump of cat-tail.

**Red-winged Blackbird**
- a handsome all-black blackbird with flashing red shoulder patches; females are brown streaked; common breeder in cat-tail marshes and wet meadows; aggressive in defence of its young and nest; an early (mid-March) migrant.

**Northern Yellowthroat**
- beautiful warbler with bright yellow underparts, greenish back and conspicuous black facial mask; females are more plainly coloured; nests in cat-tail marshes and sedge meadows where it is commonly heard singing a loud *Witchity-witchity-witch* song.

**Song Sparrow**
- a delightful brown-striped sparrow with a distinctive 'stick-pin' spot on its breast; found along grassy riverbanks, marsh edges and pond margins; a common early migrant (mid-March) with a beautifully cheery song.

**Muskrat**
- large, chunky, brownish rodent with a long, bare tail; found in cat-tail marshes; makes a lodge of a hollowed out pile of aquatic vegetation above the water; feeds exclusively on aquatic vegetation; active all year.

**Bull Frog**
- large, green or brown amphibian with a yellow throat (males); the largest Canadian frog; males bellow their loud *jug-o'-rum* breeding call from cat-tail marshes, weedy river bays and deep ponds throughout the summer.

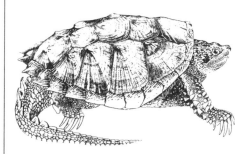

**Mink**
- large, darkly coloured weasel with a long bushy tail; an excellent swimmer that pursues fish, crustaceans and small animals on land or water; active year round in wet meadows and marshes; does not change colour in winter.

**Snapping Turtle**
- huge, prehistoric-looking reptile with powerful jaws and dinosaur-like, saw-toothed tail; inhabits weedy water in marshes, along lakes and rivers and (uncommonly) seen basking on logs or shore banks; not naturally aggressive in the water.

**Painted Turtle**
- our common "mud-turtle", with a low, smooth shell and yellow-striped face, red-striped neck and limbs and pale undersides; commonly seen basking on logs, often in large groups; feeds on small fish and invertebrates; usually lays 6 to 14 eggs in a sandy bank in the spring.

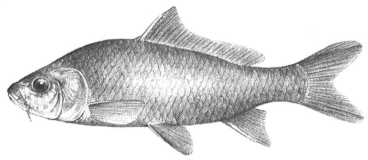

**Carp**
- large, yellowish-brown or olive-green bottom feeder; sucks up blts of plant and animal material in marshes and weedy bays; a European introduction first recorded in the Capital in the 1940's and now common in large rivershore marshes.

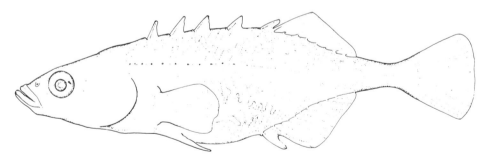

**Brook Stickleback**
- small, dark-olive minnow usually with 5 short, sharp spines along its back; found in quiet water of streams, marshes and weedy lake bays; male builds a round nest of plant material within which the female lays her eggs.

Lakes & Rivers

**Woodland Creek, Gatineau Park**
*(P. Hall)*

# LAKES & RIVERS

Just as lakes and rivers served as highways for the early European explorers seeking the natural wealth of Canada's interior, they served as migration routes for plants and animals spreading northward following the end of the last glacial period. Seeds, fragments of plants and whole organisms were carried along by water movement as well as by other travellers along the waterways. In this way large areas of Canada were repopulated by thousands of species of plants and animals. The process continues even today.

Within the water itself an array of life forms prosper. They too have responded to the changes in their habitat brought on by great natural forces; the glacial periods and subsequent invasion of the Capital area by the Champlain Sea are examples. There are pockets of habitat that remain much as they were in post-glacial times, cut off from their typical range by great distances.

Aquatic life depends upon the nature and quality of the water in which it lives, just as upland life responds to the resources available to it from the soil and vegetation. No two water bodies are precisely alike; the variety of life forms in aquatic systems here reflects that diversity.

The presence of two major geological landforms in the Capital - the Canadian Shield with its largely acidic, resistant bedrock and the sedimentary lowlands of more calcareous, softer bedrock - has great significance for aquatic systems. Canadian Shield waters are usually clear, cold, well oxygenated and low in nutrients. This is excellent for trout but low in overall biological productivity. In the warmer, nutrient rich and oxygen poor water of the lowlands, however, the high productivity results in an abundance of life such as bass, pike and a variety of aquatic plants. Such habitats are susceptible to pollution from industrial chemicals, run-off of agricultural fertilizers, storm sewer and sewage effluents and other sources that overload the aquatic environment with nutrients. While the Canadian Shield lakes and rivers are particularly susceptible to such damage, their location in the less developed Gatineau Hills has helped to limit this (so far).

Like so many natural communities, particular aquatic associations come and go with the passage of time and the forces of nature. When Beavers dam small creeks in the Gatineau Hills they create ponds that serve as habitat for particular forms of plant and animal life that eventually die out when the pond is drained or overgrown. Water levels vary tremendously throughout the year, running high in spring and lowering through the summer to a fall/early winter minimum. This all affects the temperature, rate of flow, amount of available light ... and many other subtle elements that are required by the birds, mammals, fish, turtles and insects that live here and adapt their lives accordingly.

Even in winter when a deep, solid mantle of snow and ice covers lakes and rivers, life continues underwater, albeit at a reduced level of activity. While frogs and turtles sleep away the cold in the ooze of lake bottoms, many fish continue to swim, feed and grow. At rapids where the fast water movement prevents the formation of ice, golden-eye and merganser ducks winter, feeding on these same small fish and bottom dwelling crustaceans. Our lakes and rivers, like all natural systems, never truly shut down. They may become less active for a period of time but contain life and energy at all times. They are also highly sensitive to contamination by environmental pollutants and serve as critical early warning alarms for the whole biosphere. We ignore these signals at our peril.

## Some Places to Visit

Gatineau Park
- Ramsay Lake (bog edged, acidic lake).
- Pink Lake (fresh, deep, well oxygenated lake).
- Fairy Lake (nutrient rich, warm water lake over limestone).

Leamy Lake Park
- Leamy Lake (nutrient rich, warm water lake and creek system).

McLaurin Bay
- warm water, shallow, marshy river bay.

Constance Bay Sand Hills
- Constance Bay (shallow, warm water, fresh river bay over sand).

Marlborough Forest
- throughout (beaver ponds).

Britannia Conservation Area
- Mud Lake ( over loaded, nutrient rich, warm water pond).
- Deschenes Rapids (continuously open, well oxygenated fast water).

Andrew Haydon Park
- Ottawa Beach (shallow, over loaded, sand based rivershore).

Baxter Conservation Area
- south end of trail (marshy river bay over clay).

Green's Creek Conservation Area
- Green's Creek (warm water creek in clay).
- Dominion Springs (sulphurous spring from Champlain Sea deposits).

Lower Duck Island
- offshore ( deep water, nutrient rich river channel).

Mer Bleue Conservation Area
- margin of ridges (open "moat" of acidic, boggy water surrounding bog mat and extensive beaver ponds).

**Floating Pondweed** *(Potamogeton natans)*
- long, weak-stemmed aquatic with tapered, floating leaves and a spike of dark green seeds on a separate stalk held above the water surface; in shallow to deep fresh water of streams and lakes; one of a large group of similar plants.

**Broad-leaved Arrowhead** *(Sagittaria latifolia)*
- a low plant with dark green, arrowhead-shaped leaves on tall stalks; has a central stalk supporting a number of conspicuous white flowers; grows in shallow water along river and lake shores.

**Water Plantain** *(Alisma triviale)*
- a central stalk supporting clusters of tiny white flowers arises from a group of tapering, green, shiny leaves; found on emerging mudflats of rivershores or shallow stream margins across the Capital.

**Flowering-rush** *(Butomus umbellatus)*
- tall, erect bulrush-like plant with clusters of pale pink flowers; an introduction from Eurasia first seen in the Capital about 1910 and now locally common along weedy, calcareous rivershores; still expanding its range.

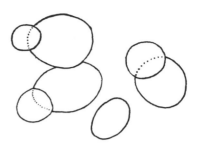

**Wild Rice** *(Zizania palustris)*
- tall, erect grass with widely spreading flower head; long narrow seeds are flattened along the upper portion of the stem; found in large stands locally in fresh, clean, flowing water in sheltered bays; an important food of ducks.

**Watermeal** *(Wolffia columbiana and W. borealis)*
- tiny, green, sticky round or oblong plants the size of sand grains; float on the surface of small pools, in marshes and other quiet, calcareous waters; expanding its range in recent years (apparently "hitch-hiking" on ducks); the world's smallest flowering plant.

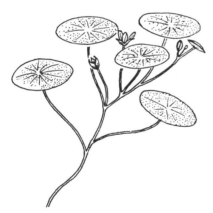

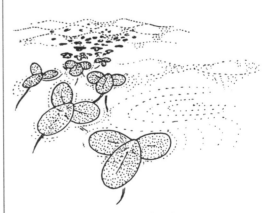

**Watershield** *(Brasenia schreberi)*
- round, reddish, floating leaves are attached in the middle to the stem; red flowers emerge on separate stalks; plants often covered in a thick, clear jelly; common especially in the Gatineau Hills, in deep, cool, fresh water.

**Duckweed** *(Lemna minor)*
- tiny, light-green pads that float on the surface and dangle a single root beneath; forms large stands covering quiet ponds, marshes and bays (often with Watermeal, above); fed upon by various aquatic birds, mammals and reptiles.

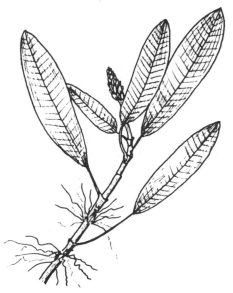

**Water Knotweed** *(Polygonum amphibium)*
- a sprawling plant with large green floating leaves connected to the stem by long, weak stalks; a spike of red flowers is held above the surface on a separate stalk; grows in groups in shallow, fresh, warm water of lakes and rivers.

**White Waterlily** *(Nymphaea odorata)*
- large, round, dark green floating leaves with reddish undersides; the beautiful white flower floats on the surface; found in fresh, clean flowing water of rivers and lakes, especially in the Gatineau Hills.

**Yellow Waterlily** *(Nuphar variegatum)*
- large, pale green, deeply cut floating leaves; a large spectacular yellow flower floats on the surface of the water; leaves and flower anchored to the massive root by long, flexible stalks; found commonly in quiet water of lakes and rivers.

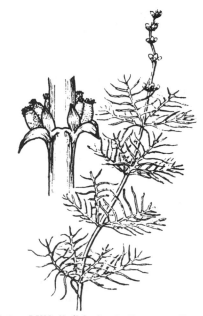

**Water Milfoil** *(Myriophyllum exalbescens)*
- long, feathery , submerged plant; leaves arise in whorls along the stem; slender spike of tiny greenish flowers emerge from the water at the stem ends; found locally in cool, fresh, deep water of rivers and lakes.

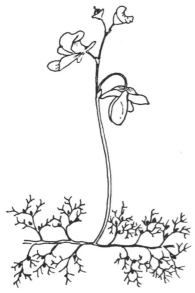

**Common Bladderwort** *(Utricularia vulgaris)*
- a floating plant with deeply dissected underwater leaves with tiny, insect-trapping bladders scattered amongst them; beautiful yellow flowers are held on a sturdy stalk emerging well above the water surface; found in quiet, shallow, water.

**Common Golden-eye**
- chunky diving duck; males are white with a black back and a green head marked by a white spot; females are grayish with brown heads; winters in large numbers at river rapids; called "whistlers" for the sound produced when flying.

**Common Merganser**
- large diving duck; males are largely white with green heads and a black back; females are grayish with rusty-brown heads; found in small groups at open water along rivers in winter; rare breeder (in hollow trees) in the Gatineau Hills.

**Lesser Scaup**
- small, diving duck with slightly peaked head shape; black-white-black pattern of male is distinctive; females are all brown except for a white patch by the bill; a common migrant and rare winter visitor of deep, fresh water; usually seen in large flocks.

**Osprey**
- huge, largely white raptor; flies with a distinctive kink in its wings; breeds in small numbers along rivers and large lakes in huge stick nests on tree tops; plunges into water from a great height in pursuit of fish.

**Herring Gull**
- slightly larger version of the Ring-billed Gull (above) but with no ring on the bill; breeds in small colonies or as pairs on islets in quiet lakes in the Gatineau Hills; becoming more common but less "weedy" than Ring-billeds.

**Ring-billed Gull**
- gray and white gull with distinctive black ring on the bill of adults; immatures are uniformly dingy brown; nests in large colonies on islands in the Chaudiere Rapids; once considered rare but now very common because of large garbage dumps.

**Spotted Sandpiper**
- small, active, brown shorebird with heavily spotted underparts in summer; nick-name "teeter-rump" is descriptive of its actions; loud "weep-weep-weep" is distinctive; common nesting bird along lake and river shores.

**Lesser Yellowlegs**
- slim, yellow-legged, grayish-brown shorebird with a long, straight bill and gray-flecked underparts; gives a characteristic "*tew-tew*" call note; a common migrant, often seen on river mud flats and silty beaches; feeds on aquatic invertebrates.

**Beaver**
- large, brown rodent with a flat, paddle shaped tail; swims (mostly at night) in ponds created by its earth and stick dam built across a stream; shelters in a large, partly hollow, stick and mud dome (lodge)out in the pond.

**Belted Kingfisher**
- chunky, bull headed blue-gray bird with a blue bar across its white chest (an additional reddish bar on females); its loud chattering call is familiar along rivers and lakeshores; hovers over then plunges into the water after small fish.

**Otter**
- large, dark, sleek carnivore with a long, narrow tail; a mostly nocturnal aquatic predator of crustaceans, small fish and other small animals along streams and in shallow lakes; seen uncommonly in the Gatineau Hills.

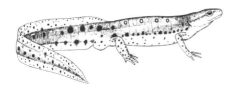

**Red-spotted Newt**
- beautiful fawn-brown or greenish aquatic salamander with black bordered red spots scattered along its sides; finned tails aid in swimming across leaf-litter covered pond and lake bottoms; red, terrestrial juvenile known as an eft.

**Map Turtle**
- large, flat-shelled reptile with an elaborate network of yellow lines on the shell and soft parts; an uncommon turtle of deep, fresh water, occasionally seen basking on deadhead logs far out in the Ottawa River; feeds mostly on molluscs.

**Northern Water Snake**
- large, blackish-brown, banded reptile with white undersides; found along weedy rivershores, in swamps, etc. feeding on small fish and amphibians; aggressive only when pestered; our most aquatic snake.

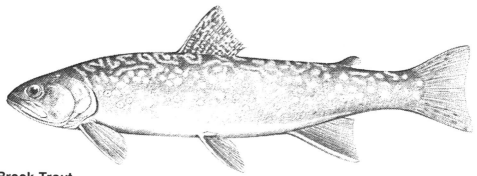

**Brook Trout**
- small, dark-green to brown; mottled above, red-centered spots on sides and a squared tail fin; found in cold, clear, oxygen-rich streams and small lakes in the Gatineau Hills; very sensitive to water pollution.

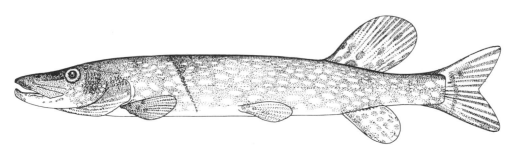

**Northern Pike**
- long, narrow bodied, green or brown fish with a distinctive duck-like snout; found in shallow, weedy areas of large lakes and rivers; a predator on smaller fish, amphibians and even Muskrats; can reach over a metre in length here.

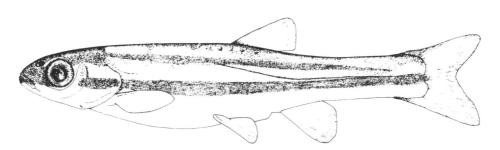

**Northern Redbelly Dace**
- beautiful pale minnow with two dark lines along the sides; males have crimson-coloured bellies in summer; found in fresh, shallow, somewhat weedy creeks and small lakes, especially in the Gatineau Hills.

116

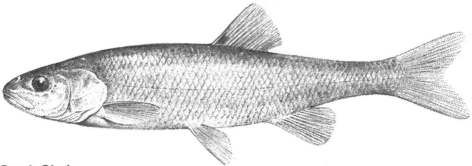

## Creek Chub
- large, silvery minnow with a dark head and a small black spot on the top fin; common in small schools in slow, fresh water of creeks and small lakes; feeds on insects and aquatic plant material.

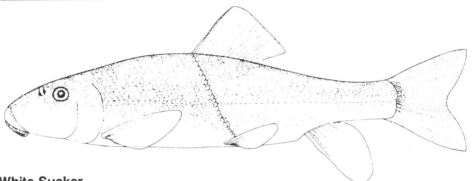

## White Sucker
- robust, blunt-nosed, silvery fish with downward-facing mouth ; found in creeks, shallow lakes and rivers, often over a mud bottom; migrates along creeks to spawn in early May; more tolerant of pollution than many species.

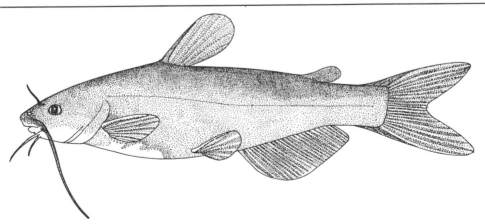

## Channel Catfish
- large, gray or black fish with distinctive catfish "whiskers" (barbels) and a forked tail; found in clean, oxygen-rich water over a sand or rock bottom ; feeds largely on small fish and invertebrates; can be over 15 kg. in Ontario.

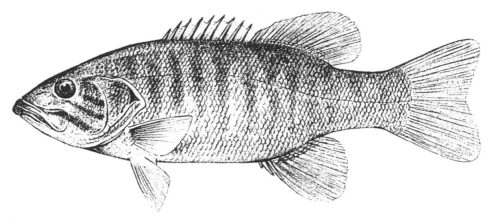

**Small-mouthed Bass**
- high backed, flat bodied greenish fish with yellowish-brown faintly barred sides; found in slow or still, shallow water; eggs are laid in a large nest scooped out of sand or gravel and defended by the male from other fish.

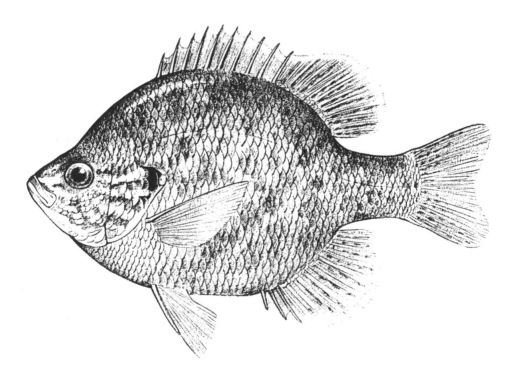

**Pumpkinseed**
- small, flat, oval bodied fish with a splotchy-brown body marked by a red and black spot on the gill cover; found commonly in dense vegetation in shallow water; male defends the scooped-out nest containing thousands of eggs.

118

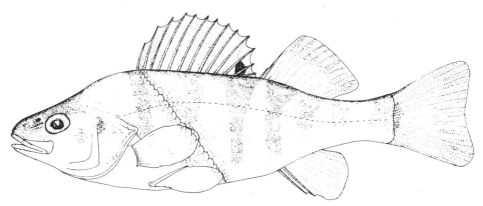

**Yellow Perch**
- small, yellowish-green fish with darker vertical bands across rough-skinned sides; found commonly in dense vegetation in shallow water throughout the Capital; feeds on insects and small invertebrates.

# PLACES TO SEE

The following section identifies a variety of places found across Canada's Capital that demonstrate a wide range of the species, activities and processes that make up the natural world in this area. From among the many that could have been selected, those described here seem particularly well suited to exploration. They are also good examples of the full range of habitats described in the previous section. I have intentionally selected public lands and easily accessible areas when choices exist . This is to minimize hazards and the possibility of unauthorized access. Some restricted areas and private lands are included, however; you must be sure of your responsibilities under trespass regulations before venturing into any area. Similarly, please be sure to respect the resources you are going to enjoy by not damaging the site or the species. It is an offense under the National Capital Act to damage or remove plants or animals from National Capital Commission lands (including the Greenbelt and Gatineau Park). It is offensive to needlessly damage or despoil the natural values of any of these areas in any case. Please refer to the DO's and DON'TS section (page 189) before your first visit to one of these areas to ensure the the the most positive experience for you and the site.

Do not assume that some local spots that you know of have no significance just because I haven't listed them; they may be just as naturally diverse as some of these. If I were to mention all -or even many - of the interesting woodlots and such in the Capital, this book would become volumes. A number of other places that are interesting but for one reason or another were not included here, are listed at the end of this section (see Other Areas page 176). By exploring some of the areas I have described however, I hope you will be able to enjoy many of the natural offerings of the Capital more fully, both here and wherever you might wish to explore.

The areas recommended for exploration (and shown on the map at the back of the book) are as follows:

## Quebec

1) Poltimore Road
2) Gatineau Park
2a) Ramsay Lake
2b) Eardley Escarpment
2c) Champlain Lookout
2d Mackenzie King Estate
2e) Old Chelsea Ravine
2f) Hickory Trail
3) Wychwood
4) Champlain Park Woods
5) Brebeuf Park
6) Tache Gardens Woods
7) Leamy Lake Park
8) Beauchamp Lake Park
9) McLaurin Bay

## Ontario

10) Carleton Place Hackberry Stand
11) Mill of Kintail Conservation Area
12) The Burnt Lands
13) Constance Bay Sand Hills
14) Carp Hills
15) Shirleys Bay
16) Stony Swamp Conservation Area
17) Stillwater Creek
18) Andrew Haydon Park
19) Britannia Conservation Area
20) Pinhey Forest Reserve
21) Carlington Woods
22) Central Experimental Farm

## Ontario (cont.)

# 1) Poltimore Road

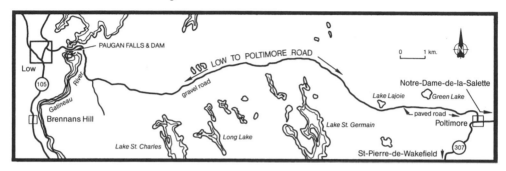

A winding gravel road twists eastward from the Paugan Falls hydro dam at Low to the village of Poltimore (Portland-Ouest) at Highway 307, a distance of just under 20 km. The landscape is variable, with large treed hills rising up from the roadside creek valley, leading eastward to a level sand plain. There are scattered houses along the road but it remains a relatively wild area of young hardwoods and spruce forest ... a very northern sort of place.

**Features:**
The Poltimore Road offers a delightful cross-section of lightly developed, conifer dominated Canadian Shield country that characterizes the northern edge of the Capital area. At the Gatineau River by Low, the spectacular Paugan Falls thunder down from the hydro dam (over which even vans can cross), exposing the pure white marble bedrock of the gorge below. This area, enriched by the lime of the marble, is an interesting spot for botanists. Eastward from the Falls typical granite hills predominate, covered by forests of birch, poplar and young maple. Dense spruce and fir forests in the sheltered, shaded valley bottom are typical along the creek. This forest mosaic changes, depending upon the slope of the hills and the history of the site and eventually spills down onto a more level plain. The plain results from the deposition of millions of tons of sand that were carried here in the meltwaters of the glaciers many centuries ago. The frequency of pine and poplar increases on the plain and remains high until the open farmlands and scrubby pastures of Poltimore are reached. This variation in habitats encourages a wide diversity of northern plants and animals that are otherwise infrequently seen in the Capital. It is especially well known as an area to find winter finches, northern hawks, woodpeckers and breeding birds.

## Visiting:
The road is open year round, but a private vehicle is essential for getting to the area. Stops can be made along the roadway in most areas and traffic is light. No public facilities are present along the route ; visitors should have sufficient gasoline and other supplies before venturing down the road.

## Equipment and Considerations:
The road is probably most interesting from a natural history standpoint in winter, but this is a time when great care must be taken with travel on quiet, slippery, back-country roads. Make sure you and your vehicle are prepared for the possibility of a winter emergency before coming here. Snowshoes are usually essential for visitors wishing to venture off the road in winter. Binoculars and a camera are desirable. To fully appreciate the winter finches (in a year when the conifer cone crop has attracted them here) some previous knowledge of the calls of the different species is useful. In summer, a tape recording of songs of breeding birds will be rewarding (see Equipment, in DO'S AND DON'TS section, page 190). The road may be in poor shape in early spring.

## Seasonal Events & Suggestions:
**Summer** - breeding birds of the Canadian Shield (especially thrushes and warblers) in June and early July.
- lush fern growth along the road and stream banks and unusual flora of the marble deposit at Paugan Falls.

**Fall & Winter** - winter finches (Evening Grosbeaks, crossbills, Purple Finches, etc.)in large numbers in years with good tree seed crops.
- resident northern birds (Common Raven, Northern Goshawk, etc.) all along road.
- uncommon northern visitors (Boreal Chickadee, Black-backed Woodpecker, etc.) in conifers along the road.

## References:
Brunton, D.F and J.D. Lafontaine. 1974. The Distribution of *Pellaea* in Quebec and eastern Ontario. Naturaliste canadien 101:937-939.

Gillett, J.M. 1972. Two New Records for Pinedrops (*Pterospora andromedea Nutt.*) for Ontario and Quebec. Canadian Field-Naturalist 86:172-175.

Roots, J. 1969. Explorer's Corner : Paugan Falls. Trail & Landscape 3:128-129.

# 2) Gatineau Park

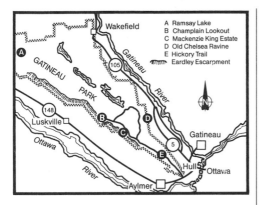

Wakefield

A Ramsay Lake
B Champlain Lookout
C Mackenzie King Estate
D Old Chelsea Ravine
E Hickory Trail
Eardley Escarpment

This 35,000 hectare area of rugged Canadian Shield in the Outaouais is a favoured and familiar locality for scenic drives, day hikes and cross-country skiing for tens of thousands of residents and visitors to Canada's Capital. In addition to its beautiful driveways, swimming beaches and interpretive facilities, Gatineau Park ilustrates the majority of natural conditions found on the southern Canadian Shield in southwestern Quebec. To introduce you to the array of Beaver ponds, maple forests, cliff systems, caves, creek valleys and meadows - to name only some of the features found here-would take a book onto itself. In this guide I have identified only a few areas, places that provide particular opportunities for understanding the Park's natural richness. I strongly suggest that you go on from here and explore this fascinating, nationally significant natural area on your own.

Gatineau Park is a federal park, managed for a variety of recreational and environmental goals by the Na-tional Capital Commission. Visitors should be careful to observe the regulations on travel and activities set by the Commission to protect the natural resources of the park.

Six places within Gatineau Park are discussed; Ramsay Lake, Eardley Escarpment, Champlain Lookout, Mackenzie King Estate, Hickory Trail and Old Chelsea Ravine.

Although references to the individual sites are listed with each, some general information on the Park as a whole is useful for visitors. There are two centers for information in the Park itself, both of which will provide information and answers to your questions:

**Old Chelsea Visitor Centre** - on the Meech Lake Road just north of Old Chelsea; open daily (year-round); phone 827-2020.

**Lac Philippe Visitor Centre** - at the entrance to Lac Philippe; open weekends (year round); phone 456-2259.

**The National Capital Commission Information Centre** at 14 Metcalfe Street in Ottawa (996-1811) can also provide information and literature (weekday business hours), including a fold-out brochure/map of the Park, a variety of floral and faunal checklists, trail maps and brochures on camping. The following describes the six areas I have singled out for discussion in Gatineau Park.

# 2a) Ramsay Lake

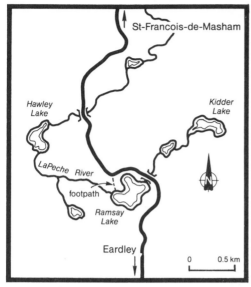

Situated just west of the Eardley to St-Francois-de-Masham Road, the lake was formerly a popular picnic and boating destination for visitors to the western end of Gatineau Park. It remains a pretty spot, set deeply into glacial sand and ringed with bog mat vegetation. The water is cold, tea-coloured (from the tannic acid of the bog)and still. The mat of living moss and bog vegetation is slowly, ever so slowly, expanding outward from the shore.

In theory it will eventually cover the pond with a solid mat and support a forest of Black Spruce and Tamarack. In reality bog rimmed lakes all across the Canadian Shield are usually kept from completing this succession by fire, wave action and the depth of the lake itself. Shallow, boggy water-bodies can commonly be found in all stages of this progression from open lake to bog forest throughout the north, however.

## Features:
The bog mat surrounding Ramsay Lake is actually floating on the water surface. It is saturated with acidic water and is very low in nutrients, thus encouraging growth of an association of unusual plants that can cope with these demanding conditions. These include insect-eating plants such as sun-dew and Pitcher-plant, as well as a variety of grasses, sedges and even orchids. The lake water itself supports a variety of un-usual plant life, including other insect-eating species and several rare aquatics. The young poplar and spruce forest that surrounds the lake contrasts strikingly with the Larch and Black Spruce of the bog mat. Few trees or shrubs are capable of surviving on this substrate of slowing decaying plant material that is continuously wet and acidic.

## Visiting:
The public picnic area, toilets, etc. have been removed and access restricted since the spring of 1987. Visitors should be prepared to walk in the short distance from the main road. Private transportation is essential and there are no services available in the area. The closest camping facilities are at Lac LaPeche to the north. A number of stores, service stations, etc. can be found on Highway 148 near Luskville to the south. The 1:50,000 topographic map (31 F/9) would be an asset.

## Equipment and Considerations:
Mosquitoes and black flies can be fierce in spring and early summer, so you should come prepared. You will get wet feet trying to get close to the bog mat (for the sake of the delicate plant life there, you should stay off it). Either wear tall boots or "bog boots"...

an old pair of sneakers that you don't mind getting wet and mucky. Viewing the bog mat from a canoe is a great way to observe the interesting life on it, as well as offering opportunities for exploring the rest of the lake. Take a camera to document the unusual plant life (a close-up capability is desirable) and bring along binoculars too ; there is no telling what might fly in or turn up in this spot.

**Seasonal Events & Suggestions:**
**Summer** - insect-eating plants and heath shrubs on the bog mat.
- unusual northern plants along the creekside mat.

**Fall** - the rare Bog Aster in profusion

along the mat.
- colour contrasts offered between upland forest hardwoods and wetland conifers.
- migrating northern birds.

**References:**
Anonymous. 1980. Gatineau Park Master Plan. National Capital Commission, Ottawa.

Brunton, D.F. 1973. The Mountain Club-moss - A Relict from the Past. Trail & Landscape 7:66-68.

Brunton, D.F. 1981. Bog Aster *(Aster nemoralis)* rediscovered in the Ottawa District. Trail & Landscape 15:130-132.

# 2b) Eardley Escarpment

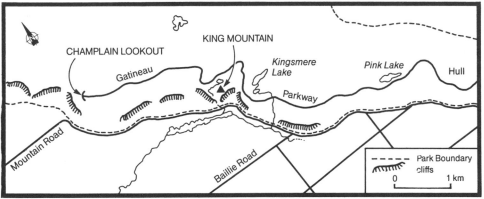

As the Canadian Shield gives way to the lowlands of the Ottawa Valley along the southern boundary of Gatineau Park, it forms a huge escarpment that runs for many kilometers to the east and west. Huge cliff-faces are located here and there where the slopes are too steep to hold enough soil for forest growth. This is clearly the most striking natural feature in the Ottawa Valley and has dictated the placement of roads, housing, railways and farming as well as the form and

behaviour of the natural flora and fauna.

**Features:**
The escarpment consists mostly of ancient, hard, acidic granite and gneiss bedrock. Its southern exposure allows for longer sunlight hours and thus, warmer than normal conditions on the cliff and cliff-top forests. This has encouraged the persistence of a number of plants from the time when the climate of the Capital was warmer

126

than it is today. So it is that unusual species occur, some in exceptional abundance. Such a large amount of exposed rock is, in itself, uncommon in the Capital area. Cliff nesting Ravens can be found year-round along the escarpment edge as a result. Up drafts create excellent soaring conditions and are used by migrating hawks and even eagles, as well as by the increasingly common Turkey Vulture. The escarpment served as the shoreline of the Champlain Sea some 11,000 years ago and plants and animals can still be found here that reflect that past.

## Visiting:
The lip of the escarpment can be visited from several viewpoints along the Gatineau Parkway . These lookouts, Champlain Lookout in particular, offer spectacular views of the cliffs and the adjacent valley floor. They are also excellent sites from which to observe migrating hawks in the fall. Good views of nesting Ravens can be had by carefully scanning the cliffs near the Champlain Lookout by binoculars from the Mountain Road in Aylmer. It is not recommended that you climb the cliffs or talus slopes in search of unusual plants as this could be very hazardous.

## Equipment and Considerations:
Viewing from the cliff-top lookouts requires no special preparation. A private vehicle is normally required for access to these sites, however. Basic toilet and parking facilities are provided and some geological interpretation is also offered by the National Capital Commission at Champlain Lookout. Climbing on the cliffs or talus should be avoided ; it is hazardous and can be very destructive to the natural vegetation. The cliffs also support large populations of Poison-

ivy. Binoculars are very important for viewing distant escarpment features and for identifying hawks and other birds flying along the cliffs. A wide-angle lens offers the best results for photographing the broad vistas displayed from the lookouts. The Gatineau Parkway is only open to vehicles in the summer months and may be restricted to non-peak periods during the height of fall colours.

## Seasonal Events & Suggestions:
**Spring** - nesting Ravens on the cliffs north of Aylmer.

**Summer** - escarpment and lowlands vista from the lookouts.
- soaring Turkey Vultures along the cliff-tops.
-interpretive trail along escarpment from Champlain Lookout.

**Fall** - spectacular autumn colours along the escarpment.
- hawk migration by the lookouts.

## References:
Brunton, D.F and J.D. Lafontaine. 1974. An Unusual Escarpment Flora in western Quebec. Canadian Field-Naturalist 88: 337-344.

Brunton, D.F. and J.D. Lafontaine. 1975. The Slender Cliff-brake in the Ottawa District. Trail & Landscape 9:40-42.

Lafontaine, J.D. 1973. Range Extension of the Blunt-lobed Woodsia, *Woodsia obtusa* (Spreng.) Torr. (Polypodiaceae), in Canada. Canadian Field-Naturalist 87:56.

Lafontaine, J.D. and D.F. Brunton. 973. The Purple Cliff-brake, *Pellaea atropurpurea* (L.)Link, in western Quebec. Canadian Field-Naturalist 86:297-298

# 2c) Champlain Lookout

**(see map for Eardley Escarpment 2b)**

Back from the lip of the Eardley Escarpment at the Champlain Lookout are several rough walking trails and one interpretive trail (complete with a brochure). They lead along old roadways or woodland tracks through a variety of upland forests and beside Beaver ponds. The natural terrain is gently rolling and tree-clad, with marble and granite outcropping here and there throughout.

**Features:**

The marble bedrock underlying much of the area enriches the soil and encourages a diverse undergrowth. This in turn offers different habitats for small mammals and birds. The area is well known for many species of breeding wood warblers - aptly called the butterflies of the bird world. Vireos, thrushes and the spectacular Scarlet Tanager are other examples of the summer birds. The forests are dominated by fine stands of Sugar Maple, with Yellow Birch and Eastern Hemlock. In lowlands and along creek valleys Beaver have built dams, creating ponds that have flooded small areas of forest. These are exceptionally active areas, with myriads of insects moving constantly about and attracting many insect eating animals. Older ponds are partially overgrown and support tiny marshes and wet meadows , some even with a Redwinged Blackbird or two. More recent ponds with deeper, open water offer occasional views of a spectacular Wood Duck or Hooded Merganser. The dying or dead trees are utilized by a variety of animals for food and shelter. Even the beautiful Redheaded Woodpecker, a rare species in the Capital, can be seen here on occasion. In winter, tracks of small rodents, weasels, Snowshoe Hare and other mammals can readily be found.

**Visiting:**

Any of the trails will offer a continuously changing picture of forest life and activity as you move from maple woods to clearings to Beaver ponds.The easiest access is from the far end of the Champlain Lookout parking lot in summer (the Parkway closes down in winter). In winter, you can ski here from a variety of trailheads further east.

**Equipment and Considerations:**

Wear sturdy foot-gear when walking the trail and bring along binoculars for a better view of the wildlife that you may encounter. Hardwood forests are usually too shady for satisfactory photography unless special measures are taken. Insect repellent will be necessary for many visitors in early summer, especially near the Beaver ponds. There are seasonal toilet facilities at the Champlain Lookout ; year-round washroom facilities are located at the Etienne Brule Lookout and at the ski shelters. Winter visits will obviously require the full complement of cross-country ski gear or snowshoes.

**Seasonal Events & Suggestions:**

**Spring** - breeding warblers and migrating forest birds in mid to late May.
- spectacular spring wildflower display throughout May.

**Summer** - rich ground flora in extensive maple forest.
- abundant breeding birds of forests

128

and Beaver ponds.
- White-tailed Deer feeding by ponds and meadows in early morning.

**Fall** - spectacular colour in the hardwood forests.

**Winter** - mammal tracks in snow.
- bird feeders at ski shelters (Western, Huron, Shilly Shally and Keogan) .

**References:**
Anonymous. (n.d.) Winter Trails : Gatineau Park. National Capital Commission, Ottawa.

Interpretation Service. 1984. Gatineau Park Interpretation Brochure: Champlain Trail. National Capital Commission, Ottawa.

Thomson, S.C. 1967. Let's Look at the Gatineau Park. (Sentier Champlain). Trail & Landscape 1:102-103.

# 2d) Mackenzie King Estate

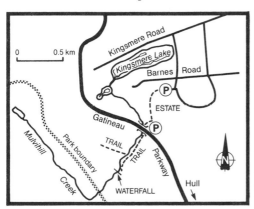

The grounds of the summer estate of the late Prime Minister Mackenzie King are best known for the bizarre collection of ruins he assembled there. Although tended lawn and buildings are most evident, interesting natural corners remain. The estate is situated on marble bedrock and slopes southward to the lip of the Eardley Escarpment, where a rich, interesting hardwood forest can be visited along a delightful path.

**Features:**
Mulvihill Creek tumbles across the estate, under the Parkway and then over the lip of the escarpment with a great noise and a spray of cool water. Along

its steep valley walls rich, loamy soils have developed. The spring wildflower show here is possibly unrivalled anywhere in the Outaouais ; the rich, limy soils and southern exposure combine to encourage an abundance of blooms, often well in advance of those at lower elevations near Ottawa. Large and handsome Sugar Maple, Yellow Birch and Eastern Hemlock are common along the creekside trail. Purple-fringed Orchids can be found at loops in the creek by the Ostrich Fern beds in early summer. A constant play of bird song from the hardwoods all along the trail mixes with the music of the creek and later, with that of the falls.

**Visiting:**
This is the sort of place where you can spend a half an hour or half a day. The trail from the lower estate parking lot turns under the Parkway through a large culvert, then follows the creek before branching to the west along the escarpment lip. or straight on to a lookout at the water falls. The western branch is best for early spring wildflowers; the central course produces the best bird song. The trail is not accessible for the dis-

abled (though nearby Mulvihill Lake Trail is, as are the facilities at the Mackenzie King Estate). It is an easy trail to follow and well surfaced, though rather steep at the escarpment edge. Access is feasible only in the summer. Full facilities, including a delightful tea room and very interesting historical displays, are available from l0 am to 5 pm daily through the summer months at the King Estate above the parking lot.

**Equipment and Considerations:**
Sneakers or other casual foot wear are satisfactory for this trail; the creek is bridged where needed and the culvert has a dry, wooden floor. Although mosquitoes can be bad along the creek, there is little or no Poison-ivy along the trail. Binoculars are useful for observing forest birds.

**Seasonal Events & Suggestions:**
**Spring** - Woodcock courtship song and flight at dusk in April amongst the ruins (beware of Prime Ministerial spirits!).
- spectacular spring wildflowers along the trail from mid-April through May.
- small forest bird migration (warblers, vireos, etc.).

**Summer** - rich maple - birch - hemlock forest and associated ground flora.
- scenic appeal of the Mulvihill Creek waterfall.

**Fall** - beautiful autumn colours of the hardwoods.

**References:**
No specific literature is available for the trail although the National Capital Commission has program brochures on the King Estate and the interpretive program there.

# 2e) Old Chelsea Ravine

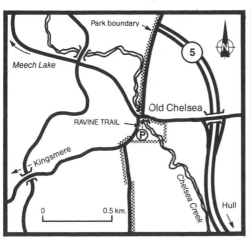

Right at the boundary of the Park and very close to the village of Old Chelsea, Chelsea Creek tumbles through a deep ravine cut deep into granite and marble. A steep trail winds down to

the ravine bottom and into a lush, green, almost magical scene.

**Features:**
The mature forest cover and creek spray maintain a cool, moist microclimate throughout the summer in the bottom of the ravine. Aside from its unusual beauty - a real sylvan gem - the ravine illustrates how dramatically conditions can vary within different forest situations. Naturalists have been drawn here since the 1880's and some of the unusual rock ferns found in the bottom of the ravine by these pioneers are still present (and are protected by law).

**Visiting:**
A good but steep walking trail runs the short distance from the picnic area

130

parking lot off the Kingsmere Road by Old Chelsea to the bridge crossing Chelsea Creek in the ravine bottom. The trail is not maintained in winter. Full commercial services, including restaurants, a gas station and a store, are available in Old Chelsea less than a kilometre away.

### Equipment and Considerations:
Casual foot wear (sneakers, loafers, etc.) are satisfactory for walking down into the ravine along the trail. Tougher gear will be required for exploration in the rougher country around it. Binoculars are an asset here and in spring when light levels are high, a

camera will be appreciated, too.

### Seasonal Events & Suggestions:
**Spring** - ground and rock flora.

**Summer** - cool, moist ravine-bottom with rushing creek.
- dramatic variation in microclimate and vegetation from top to bottom of the ravine.
- unusual creekside flora (including rare grasses).

### References:
None.

# 2f) Hickory Trail

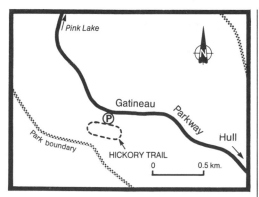

While much of Gatineau Park is dominated by fine forests of medium-aged or mature trees, large areas exhibit younger forest cover or no cover at all. Hickory Trail winds through such an area where fields are giving way to young forest. The richness of the site is enhanced by its relatively low elevation along the Eardley Escarpment, its southern exposure and relatively fertile soil. The Trail offers easy access to a complex area with a diverse and interesting plant life.

### Features:
The trail offers an excellent opportunity to experience the dramatic difference in life forms, sounds and appearance between young, scrubby forest (on the west loop) and mature, rich hardwoods (on the east loop). As the whole trail is only 0.5 km long, this can be accomplished in short order ; interpretive signs along the way describe all this very well. South of the trail along an unmarked but distinct track you can come across the open areas of overgrowing pasture that are not converted to tree cover yet. The change here is rapid ; in less than 15 years I have seen this area evolve from open, shrubby fields with scattered sumac bushes and small cherry clumps to a young forest with scattered clearings of various sizes. The large marble boulders that once dominated the vista (one of which is encountered along the western loop of the trail) are very difficult to spot now. In another 15 years, the landscape will be even further transformed.

A number of southern plant species that are uncommon or rare in the Park are found here; the Bitternut Hickory for which the trail is named (and which is well described on the eastern loop) is an example of this group. So too is the huge Bitternut tree in the right hand side of the track through the clearings to the south of the trail. When tent caterpillar numbers are high, this is a good place to hear and possibly see Black-billed Cuckoo. Eastern Phoebes often nest on the rafters of the picnic area washrooms, as do Field Sparrows, a locally common species, in the scrubby clearing to the south.

### Visiting:
The Hickory Trail is a self-guiding interpretive trail, with instructive display panels along the route that describe important natural features. It is accessible for disabled persons as the trail is wide, level and surfaced with rock crush. Access to the site is by private vehicle only.

### Equipment and Considerations:
The site is well serviced, with parking, picnic tables and washrooms all at hand. No special preparations are required for walking the short Hickory Trail, although sturdy foot-gear is advisable when venturing in the scrubby fields south of the picnic area. There is no Poison-ivy along the trail and biting insects are not severe in this dry area.

### Seasonal Events and Suggestions:
**Spring** - spring flora in the mature hardwoods.
- migrating birds in the younger forest.

**Summer** - comparison of young growth and mature maple forest vegetation and flora.
- common breeding birds of various woodland and clearing habitats.

**Fall** - rock plants on the marble boulders.
- autumn colour in the sumac groves and hardwoods.

### References:
Brunton, D.F. and J.D. Lafontaine. 1974. An Unusual Escarpment Flora in Western Quebec. Canadian Field-Naturalist 88: 337-344.

# 3) Wychwood (Blueberry Point)

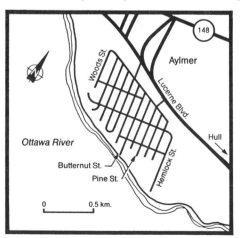

This woodland situated along the Ottawa River at Lake Deschenes has been visited by naturalists for over a century. In the early days Blueberry Point, as it was then known, was a place to see plants and animals of the coniferous forests of more northern areas. It is much the same today.

### Features:
Many of the floral and faunal elements of the vast pineries of the upper Ottawa Valley are evident here. The White Pine that is dominant in Wych-

wood offers shelter and food to various species of finches in winter, including Evening Grosbeaks and crossbills. Many birds nest here, including the locally uncommon Pine Warbler. Migrating waterfowl can be observed on Lake Deschenes from access points in both spring and fall; the woods can be crowded with migrating forest birds at this time. This has been a particularly good place to observe woodpeckers, including the spectacular Pileated Woodpecker.

### Visiting:
Access from Boulevard Lucerne (the lower Aylmer Road) via Pine Street (appropriately enough!) is direct. Access to Lake Deschenes for viewing waterfowl is available from the south end of Butternut Street. As the area is all private land in which many houses and summer cottages are maintained, roads are kept open year-round.

### Equipment and Considerations:
This is a residential area in Aylmer and the private property rights of residents must be observed. Visitors should stay along the roadways unless given permission to enter by land owners. The land is quite level and offers easy walking. Binoculars are important for observing bird life. A spotting scope is very helpful in scanning the lake for waterfowl. There is lots of Poison-ivy here and biting insects can be bad in early summer, so take the appropriate precautions.

### Seasonal Events & Suggestions:
**Spring** - Pine Warblers singing in late April.
- bird migration near the lake shore in the pines.

**Summer** - pine forest ground flora and vegetation.

**Fall** - migrating waterfowl along Lake Deschenes.

**Winter** - winter finches and woodpeckers in the pines.

### References:
Reddoch, J.M. 1979. Favorite OFNC Excursion Sites in the 19th Century. Trail & Landscape 13:71-96.

# 4) Champlain Park Woods

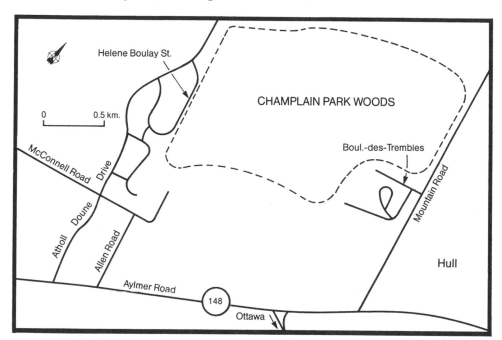

North and east of the Champlain Bridge in Aylmer and Hull a fine sandy woodland occupies an area of low to level ground. A series of trails running through it offers excellent access to a pleasant woodland setting.

## Features:
Much of the woods is medium-aged to mature Sugar Maple forest with clumps of Eastern Hemlock and numerous Beech trees throughout. Younger forests of White Birch, Trembling Aspen and Balsam Fir intermix with this where the soil varies from dry to moist, offering a variety of habitats for plants and animals. The natural diversity of the woods is at a high level and gives visitors the chance to encounter a large number of woodland plants and animals typical of Canada's Capital.

## Visiting:
Walking, horse and ski trails all run through the woods. The National Capital Commission, the land manager, maintains two cross-country ski trails (7.3 kms) that depart from the Champlain Golf Course parking lot ; the other trails are not maintained. Parking is available on side roads adjacent to the woods ; there are no public facilities.

## Equipment and Considerations:
Sturdy walking-gear is recommended for the trails. They are relatively level but can be wet and rough in spots. Binoculars are useful for observing birds and mammals. The light levels are often too low for satisfactory photography in the woods, though there is no end of subjects if one has the equipment and knowledge to cope with this limitation. This would be an excellent place for a snowshoe

outing, as well as being available for cross-country skiing.

**Seasonal Events & Considerations**:
**Summer** - common wildflowers and ferns of the Capital area well represented.
- typical woodland breeding birds present.

**Fall -** rich late-summer and fall woodland flora, especially ferns of the Canadian Shield.

**Winter** - common winter residents, including grouse, woodpeckers and

owls, in the woods.
- tracks of mammals evident in the snow.

**References:**
Brunton, D.F. 1984. Nature Reserve Potential and Management in the National Capital Region. Conservation Studies 29, National Capital Commission, Ottawa.

Gagnon, D. 1980. Inventaire des Ressources Naturelles des Boises de la Region de Hull. Conservation Section, National Capital Commission, Ottawa.

# 5) Brebeuf Park

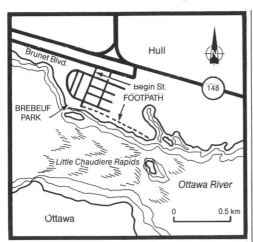

Canada's interior.

Situated in Hull on the north side of the little Chaudiere Rapids of the Ottawa River, the park provides easy access to an area where waterfowl are active year-round and where unusual plants line the shore. A national historic site marks a section of the voyageurs' portage around the Chaudiere Rapids. Visitors can literally walk in the footsteps of Champlain, Thompson, the Jesuit Fathers, LaVerendrye and the thousands of anonymous voyageurs who played such a vital role in the development of

**Features:**
A scrubby forest of hardwoods is perched on exposed limestone outcroppings along the rivershore. These disturbed woods have a high diversity of plant life, both native and introduced. The rough trail that picks its way eastward through limestone bedrock shelves and boulders can give you a new appreciation for what it must have been like to haul heavy freighter canoes over this route hundreds of years ago. Provincially rare plants like the Fragrant Sumac shrub and Hackberry tree are found all along this rugged shore. In the river large numbers of wintering ducks can be seen. These are mostly Common Goldeneye, mergansers and Black Ducks, but rare species such as Harlequin Duck and Barrow's Golden-eye are seen here on occasion. A huge and growing Ring-billed Gull colony has developed on the islands off Squaw Bay in recent years and the blizzard of breeding gulls can be plainly seen from shore.

**Visiting:**
The area is public land, partly municipal and partly federal (National Capital Commission). Access from Begin Street in Val Tetreault is good year-round, though fewer parking spots are available in winter and no clearing of trails occurs then.
The walkway to the historic plaque is paved ; the trail beyond is rough and narrow. A bicycle path from the east end of Bourget Street continues eastward in the Squaw Bay area. There are no facilities in the Park. A boulder at the trail head marks the start of the old portage and serves as the base for the historic plaque.

**Equipment and Considerations:**
Binoculars or a spotting telescope are important for observing ducks and gulls on the river. Sturdy foot-gear should be worn when travelling along the old portage trail and you should be careful to avoid the abundant Poison-ivy on the outcrops. The moist spray from the rapids in winter can chill you to the bone very quickly so dress warmly at that time. A camera to document the beautiful scenery (including fine views of the parliament area of Ottawa) and the important historic features of the place is useful.

**Seasonal Events & Suggestions:**
**Spring** - large numbers of several species of gulls roosting here at break-up.

**Summer** - large numbers of breeding gulls on the islands off Squaw Bay.
- unusual shrubs and trees along the trail by the river shore.

**Fall** - historic interest of walking the voyageurs' portage.
- rich ground flora along the trail.

**Winter** - wintering waterfowl in the rapids and along the shore.

**References:**
Brunton, D.F. 1984. Nature Reserve Potential and Management in the National Capital Region. Conservation Studies 29, National Capital Commission, Ottawa.

Gagnon, D. 1980. Inventaire des Boises de la Region de Hull. Conservation Section, National Capital Commission, Ottawa.

# 6) Tache Gardens Woods

The woods are situated in a broad valley sloping southward across western Hull towards the Ottawa River. A variety of topography and vegetation types combined with a slightly warmer-than-normal microclimate, have encouraged a diverse and unusual flora to develop. The site is managed by the National Capital Commission and has been identified as being an important natural area of the Capital.Features:
The limestone bedrock that is so close to the surface and which outcrops in some places has encouraged a number of rare lime-loving plant species. These include the Black Maple, a magnificent tree that is considered to be rare in the province of Quebec. Two other species (an orchid and a sedge) are also listed as being provincially rare. Much of the area is a rich mixture of hardwood and young coniferous forest cover. An overgrowing pasture in the north of the area is rich in summer breeding birds. Disturbance to the woodlands is light elsewhere. A small White Cedar swamp adds an ad-

ditional habitat. This is a good place in which to become familiar with some of the Capital's uncommon woodland plant species.

**Visiting:**
North from Lacasse Street in Hull a trail runs from a pedestrian gate into the woods. A wide but informal trail also enters the woods from the east, by the parking lot of the Hull jail. Trails through the area are mostly wide and easy to follow, if steep in some places. Parking is available along adjacent side streets; there are no facilities in the woods area itself.

**Equipment and Considerations:**
Normal walking gear will do though you should be aware of the abundant Poison-ivy along the trail edges and throughout the more open woodland areas. Biting insects may be a problem in late spring and early summer. A botanical field guide is useful. Snowshoes are recommended in winter.

**Seasonal Events & Suggestions:**
**Spring** - wildflower display (May - early June)

**Summer** - unusual woodland plant species.
- common breeding birds of scrubby pasture.

**Fall** - rich fall flora, especially asters and goldenrods.
- White-tailed Deer in the valley.

**Winter** - mammal tracks in snow.

**References:**
Brunton, D.F. 1984. Nature Reserve Potential and Management in the

National Capital Region. Conservation Studies 29, National Capital Commission, Ottawa.

Gagnon, D. 1980. Inventaire des Ressources Naturelles des Boises de la Region de Hull. Conservation Section, National Capital Commission, Ottawa.

# 7) Leamy Lake Park South

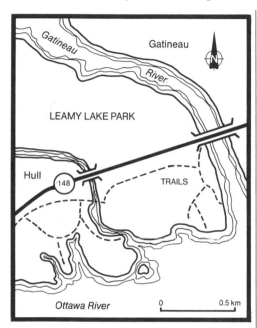

This area of National Capital Commission land is situated on the outwash material deposited by thousands of years of water flow at the mouth of the Gatineau River. It has developed a mature and distinctive forest cover that has changed little since Samuel de Champlain passed these woods over 350 years ago. North of Highway 148 the park is more developed and recreationally oriented.

## Features:
This is an ancient lowland forest, dominated by massive Silver Maples. Black Ash, White Elm and the provincially rare Hackberry are locally common. Basswood and Bur Oak dominate on drier knolls where the undergrowth is well developed. While the ground vegetation is sparse under the maples (largely as a result of yearly spring flooding), it forms an association that took many decades to develop and one which is not seen in younger swamp forests in the Capital. These Silver Maple swamps are perhaps as pristine as any area in Canada's Capital. That situation is all the more remarkable at a site in the center of a large metropolitan area.

## Visiting:
The margins of the swamp forest are easily reached along the recreational pathways from Leamy Lake Park north of Highway 148, where parking, picnic facilities and washrooms are available. Branches off the pathways go out into the swamp forest to viewpoints on the Gatineau and Ottawa Rivers and serve as good access points to the swamp area.

## Equipment and Considerations:
Rubber boots will be necessary if you wish to keep your feet dry while exploring the swamp forest off the pathways; they also are reasonable protection against the Poison-ivy that is common in places here. Insect repellent will certainly be necessary for most visitors in late spring and early summer as protection against the hordes of mosquitoes. This is really a place for the more advanced naturalist, but the casually interested visitor can get a sense of the majesty of the forest

138

from travelling along the pathways. The lush green scenery within the forest is highly photogenic.

**Seasonal Events & Suggestions:**
**Spring-** canoeing through the forest during spring flood.
- chorus of singing amphibians at night in April.

**Summer-** rich Silver Maple forest and ground flora.
- breeding Wood Ducks in sloughs.

**Fall-** unusual flora on knolls and in sloughs.
- forest colour in the maple swamp.

**References:**
Brunton, D.F. 1984. Nature Reserve Potential and Management in the National Capital Region. Conservation Studies 29, National Capital Commission, Ottawa.

Gagnon, D. 1980. Inventaire des Ressources Naturelles des Boises de la Region de Hull. Conservation Section, National Capital Commission, Ottawa.

MacDonald, M. 1947. The birds of Brewery Creek. Oxford University Press, Toronto.

# 8) Beauchamp Lake Park

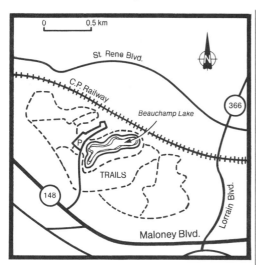

This regional park offers year-round access into a complex and beautiful area of Canadian Shield outcrop. The outcrop is surrounded by the softer, younger limestone rock. Beauchamp Lake is the focus of the park, providing areas of recreational and natural interest for visitors.

**Features:**
Beauchamp Lake is typical of many small, picturesque Shield lakes. Along its shores and especially to the south, young hardwoods are developing amongst bare granite bedrock areas. This contrast in habitats offers opportunities for a wide variety of plants and animals, some of which are more typical of areas to the north and east in Quebec. The provincially rare Poison Sumac (a close relative of the equally disagreeable Poison-ivy) is found along the lakeshore. This is the only site in which it has been discovered in the Capital and is a biogeographic oddity. Forests of Sugar Maple and other hardwood species occur to the west of the lake.

**Visiting:**
The road from Maloney Boulevard (Highway 148) is kept open year-round and leads to large parking areas. Full swimming, picnicing and snack-bar facilities are maintained near the parking lots in summer. An extensive system of ski trails fan out

from parking lots and a heated shelter is maintained in winter. From June to September there is a parking fee, presently amounting to $3.00 (1987).

### Equipment and Considerations:
The area is well serviced. Only regular walking gear is necessary in summer along the trails. More durable footgear is recommended if you want to explore the rock areas to the south and east of the lake. Be careful when travelling north of the swimming beach along the lakeshore where the Poison Sumac is located ; it is every bit as toxic as Poison-ivy.

### Seasonal Events & Suggestions:
**Spring**- wildflowers in the hardwoods west of the lake.
- migrant forest birds in the woods and scrublands.

**Summer**- typical Shield plants of southern Quebec on the outcrops.
- breeding warblers in the hardwoods.

**Fall** - unusual eastern flora (especially aster family) on the outcrops.
- fall colours in the woodland and scrub areas.

**Winter**- mammal tracks along the ski trails.
- winter shrub and tree identification opportunities.

### References:
Raymond, M. 1950. Esquisse Phytogeographique du Quebec. Memoires du Jardin Botanique de Montreal 5, Montreal. (see Poison Sumac, *Rhus vernix* ).

# 9) McLaurin Bay

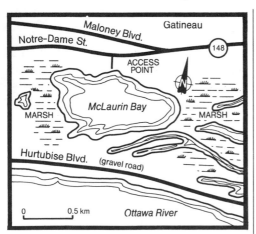

Situated a few kilometers east of Templeton in Gatineau along the north shore of the Ottawa River, this water body was originally a river bay. Aquatic and wetland vegetation has grown in to such a degree that it essentially has become a distinct, shal-

low water lake. The aquatic life of the lake is abundant in this warm, nutrient rich water. It offers a good day outing for exploring the diversity of aquatic life along the Ottawa River.

### Features:
The large bull-rush and cat-tail marshes of the lake have been explored by naturalists for over a century, providing many examples of the species that thrive in rich, shallow water river marshes. Shallow water feeding ducks and geese use the lake as a resting and feeding area in migration as well. A typical ash-elm-oak rivershore forest occupies the dry sandy shore along Hurtubise Boulevard, from where you can scan a large stretch of the Ottawa River. This would serve as a good place to observe migrating waterfowl or from which to travel out to Lower Duck Is-

land (see page 170).

river and in the marshes.

**Visiting:**
A small gravel track from Notre-Dame Street leads to a boat launch area at the northwest corner of the lake. Hurtubise Boulevard offers access to the Ottawa River shore but does not extend as far east as the lake. This is a summer area. Parking at the boat launch is quite limited.

**Seasonal Events & Suggestions:**
**Spring** - migrant waterfowl along the

**Summer** - night chorus of frogs and marsh birds.
- rich aquatic and marsh vegetation.

**Fall** - interesting plant species along the Ottawa River shoreline.

**References:**
None.

# 10) Carleton Place Hackberry Stand

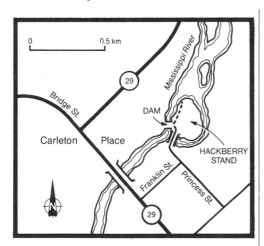

A narrow strip of rocky woodland in downtown Carleton Place along the Mississippi River harbours a grove of this rare southern tree. The site is a picturesque one alongside a set of rapids and is a pleasant place to visit summer or winter.

**Features:**
The focus of the site is the stand of Hackberry trees *(Celtis occidentalis)* that dominates the forest of medium aged hardwoods. This southern tree is found rarely in large numbers in the Capital; only the Duck Islands (see page 170) support as many in-

dividuals. The stand supports a number of other southern species as well, including the Hairy Rye-grass *(Elymus villosus)* that was until recently considered to be rare in Canada. It is also known for the unusual insects found there. Wild Garlic *(Alliaria petiolata)* an alien species, has recently invaded the undergrowth and is threatening to smother native species. The water of the adjacent rapids is open year-round and is often home to wintering ducks or even a Belted Kingfisher.

**Visiting:**
A somewhat rough footpath runs along the rivershore from the bridge. Parking is available on side streets or (for a few vehicles) by the start of the trail. There are no facilities at the site although downtown Carleton Place is only a few hundred meters away.

**Equipment and Considerations:**
A camera is highly desirable as the rapids, general landscape and knobby barked, twisted, gray forms of the Hackberry trees all offer fine subjects. Sturdy footgear is recommended. Poison-ivy is abundant, both on the trail and throughout the woods. There

141

are no restraints along the steep rock face over the rapids so small children should not be left on their own.

**Seasonal Events & Suggestions:**
**Spring** - flowering Hackberry trees and wildflowers in early May.

**Summer** - fully developed Hackberry stand and ground flora.

**Winter** - wintering waterbirds along the rapids
photographic opportunities in the woods and along the river.

**References:**
Anonymous. 1973. Carleton Place boasts rare hackberry grove. Ottawa Journal, February 20.

# 11) Mill of Kintail Conservation Area

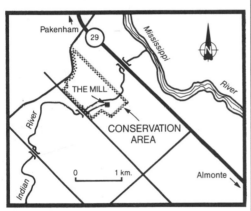

The Mill of Kintail is an historic structure housing the studio of the sculptor Robert T. Mckenzie. The Mississippi Valley Conservation Authority maintains a museum in the mill dedicated to his life and work and operates interpretive and environmental education programs on the surrounding property. The Conservation Area is set in rolling land through which the Indian River runs and includes a fine mix of woodland, cropland and wetland. There are many opportunities for hiking and exploring in this attractive setting.

**Features:**
Much of the area is covered by Sugar Maple forest in rich loamy soil. Pockets of Eastern Hemlock, White Cedar

and Yellow Birch occur within it, with White Cedar swamps and wet thickets in the lowlands. Bur Oak, Basswood and Green Ash woods are found on drier areas. The Mill of Kintail is situated on the banks of the Indian River and has become almost a 'must' visit each fall for many Ottawa Valley residents. The colour in the maple woods at this time is exceptional. The maple woods are excellent examples of the richness and diversity of the forests that once covered much of the Capital. They support a number of unusual plant species, including Black Maple and the colourful Zig-zag Goldenrod *(Solidago caesia)*. Over 200 plant species are reported from the Mill area, with many more certain to be found. The uncommon Two-lined Salamander is found along the Indian River and the common species of woodland and meadow amphibians and reptiles are well represented. The mature hardwoods are rich in breeding birds that are often associated with the Shield country of the Gatineau Hills, including the spectacular Scarlet Tanager.

**Visiting:**
Throughout the summer, parking and public washrooms are available near the Mill building. A delightful walking trail runs north from the Mill over the

river by a footbridge and into the hardwoods beyond. A ski trail provides winter access to the same woods from a parking area 1/2 km beyond the Mill entrance road. Conservation Area signs will direct you to the Mill site from Highway 15 between Pakenham and Almonte.

## Equipment and Considerations:

The trail is easy to walk in summer in regular out-door footwear. Mosquitoes can be challenging in late spring and early summer along the river, however. A wildflower field guide, binoculars and a camera would certainly be assets here.

## Seasonal Events & Suggestions:

**Spring** - spectacular Spring-beauty *(Claytonia caroliniana)* in late April - early May.
- chorus of migrating forest birds.
- raging Indian River at peak flood .

**Summer**- rich ground flora of the maple woods.
- Two-lined Salamanders along the river.
- scarlet Cardinal Flower *(Lobelia cardinalis)* along the river in August.

**Fall -** colourful hardwood forest.
- ground flora in the maple bush and along the river.

**Winter** - winter mammal tracks and typical winter birds along the ski trail.
- Porcupine denning trees in the hardwood forest.

## References:

For further information on the facilities at the Mill of Kintail Conservation Area and their interpretive programs, call the Mississippi Valley Conservation Authority in Lanark at 1-800-267-1659 or the Mill of Kintail Conservation Area office at 256-3610 (long distance from Ottawa).

# 12) The Burnt Lands

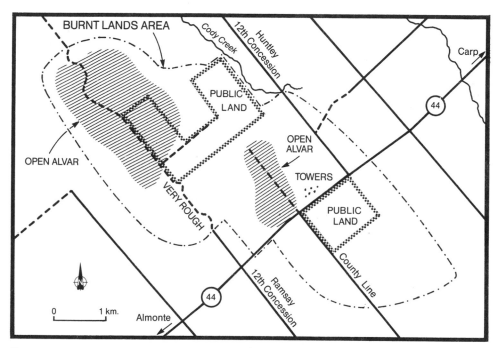

**Centered** on Highway 44 just east of Almonte and extending well back to the north and south of the road is a flat limestone plateau that supports a most extraordinary natural environment. Though much of the area has been disturbed by housing developments and some by quarry operations, large portions remain in a near-natural state. The site has been designated as an Area of Natural and Scientific Interest (ANSI) by the Ontario government which controls two large blocks of land, the other portions being privately owned. Although rather uninspiring at first glance this area is really one of the most interesting natural complexes in Canada's Capital and is one of great natural beauty as well.

**Features:**

When the land of the lower Ottawa Valley began to emerge from the frigid waters of the Champlain Sea, one of the first areas to break the surface is what we now call the Burnt Lands. A flora and fauna was established that reflected the subarctic climate of 11,000 years ago. Similar areas of vegetation elsewhere in the Capital were taken over by plants more capable of coping with modern conditions but some relict species and plant communities from that time persist at the Burnt Lands. Most important are the alvars, natural spring-flooded meadows in thin soil and on bare rock flats that have been kept open by centuries of fire. Much of the plant life and many of the insects are relicts of the cold seashore habitat of long ago. Some are beautiful wildflowers like the Yellow Lady's-slipper *(Cypripedium calceolus),* while others are less visually impressive grasses and sedges. The Burnt Lands is one of the largest examples of alvar habitat in Ontario and the only large example of this rare habitat east of the Kingston area.

Mixed forests of spruce, fir, poplar and birch are constantly - if very slowly - spreading out over them. Wetland coniferous forests support large numbers of northern plants and some breeding birds, including the musically spectacular Hermit Thrush. There also is a strong western influence in the vegetation here, reflecting its prehistoric past and connections. This is a mixing ground of northern, southern and western plants and insects.

### Visiting:

Access is easiest from Highway 44 east of Almonte and along the (gravel) county line between Ramsay and Huntley Townships. The largest alvar area is about 3 km north of the end of Concession 12 (Ramsay) along a very rough dirt track; this route is not recommended for those concerned about scratching the paint on their cars! The easiest way to see many of the features of the Burnt Lands is to explore the block of Ontario government land south of Highway 44 and east of the county line, or federal land north of the highway and west of the radio towers.

### Equipment and Considerations:

Much of the land in this area is privately owned and you should seek owner approval before venturing onto such properties. The government lands (except the fenced-in area by the radio towers) and road allowances are open to public travel, however. As the ground is often wet and muddy, especially in the spring sturdy, waterproof footwear is advised. It can become extremely hot on the open alvar in midsummer (over 45 degrees C at ground level on hot, sunny days); morning and evening visits are advisable. Deer flies are painfully common, so wear a hat. Poison-ivy is abundant. Binoculars are useful for observing bird life and for improving distant views across the alvar meadows. There is active hunting for deer and grouse in this area each fall, so be careful!

### Seasonal Events & Suggestions:

**Spring** - unusual alvar meadow flora.
- Yellow Lady's-slippers in profusion along woodland edges in June.
- spring chorus of breeding birds from mid-May to mid-June.

**Summer** - northern flora in the coniferous woodlands.
- breeding colony of rare Clay-colored Sparrows northwest of the radio towers.
- rich variety of butterflies on the alvar meadows.

**Fall** - rich alvar meadow vegetation and flora (especially along Ramsay Concession Road 12).
- diverse plant life in mixed and broad-leaved forest habitats.

### References:

Brunton, D.F. 1986. A Life Science Inventory of the Burnt Lands. Parks Branch, Ontario Ministry of Natural Resources, Kemptville. (Unpublished report).

White, D.J. 1979. Burnt Lands Alvar. Trail & Landscape 13: 34-38.

# 13) Constance Bay Sand Hills

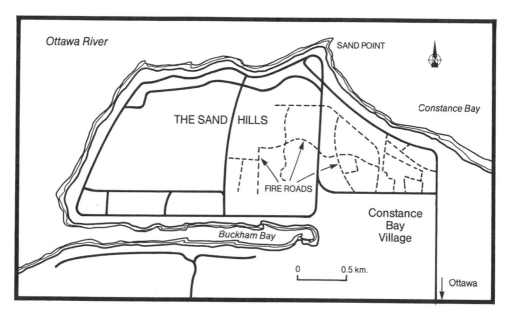

The Sand Hills are, as their name implies, a series of low hills of sand. They are situated adjacent to the Ottawa River shore in northern West Carleton Township and are owned by the township. The Ontario Ministry of Natural Resources manages the area and is responsible for extensive planting of Jack Pine trees as a means of stabilizing the sand. The area is completely surrounded by residential development. The Hills - actually fossil dunes - support a number of regionally rare plants and animals. Despite the degree of disruption to its ecological processes it remains an important natural area.

**Features:**
Sand deposited by the giant river that occupied much of the Ottawa Valley following the last glacial period was shaped by subarctic winds into dunes. Advancing plant growth stabilized the dunes centuries ago, permitting associations of sand loving plants to thrive here. Natural fire occurred on a regular basis, ensuring that some open ground was always present for the plants and animals that inhabited such sites. Plants that are relicts from these ancient conditions have been found in the Hills and despite the loss of habitat caused by the dense Jack Pine plantation and the prevention of fire, some remain. Ironically, some persist perilously on the disturbed shoulders of fire roads, tracks established to help prevent a form of disturbance that would create much more suitable habitat. One of these is the yellow flowered Puccoon (*Lithospermum carolinense*). It was likely brought here centuries ago by indians and was first reported by Samuel de Champlain in 1613. In addition to these unusual plants a number of butterflies rarely seen in the Capital are regularly found here.

146

**Visiting:**

The network of unsurfaced fire roads off the Constance Bay cottage roads offers excellent access into the Sand Hills ; it is best to leave your car along the township roads and walk in as the fire roads are intended for emergency vehicle traffic only.

**Equipment and Considerations:**

Although walking along the fire roads is easy (though not well suited for access by the disabled because of the soft roadbed), it can be very hot in the woods in mid-summer. You might consider visiting the Hills in morning or evening instead. The mosquitoes are fierce in early spring. There are no facilities maintained in the areas although a small bakery and stores are to be found in the cottage community. Bring along a camera in mid-summer to capture some of the spectacular wildflowers ; binoculars are a great help in observing the birds and butterflies along the fire roads.

**Seasonal Events & Suggestions:**

**Spring-** flowering violets and Sand Cherry along the fire roads.
- uncommon butterflies in the pine woods.

**Summer** - sand loving plants, including Puccoon, in flower along the roads.

**References:**

Layberry, R.A. *et al.* 1982. Butterflies of the Ottawa District. Trail & Landscape 16:3-59.

OMNR. 1984. Constance Bay Sand Hills : Vegetation Study, Fall, 1983. Ontario Ministry of Natural Resources, Kemptville (Unpublished report).

Porsild, A.E. 1941. A Relic Flora on Sand Dunes from the Champlain Sea in the Ottawa Valley. Canadian Field-Naturalist 55: 66-72.

White, D.J. 1979. The Sand Hills. Trail & Landscape 13:126-131.

# 14) Carp Hills

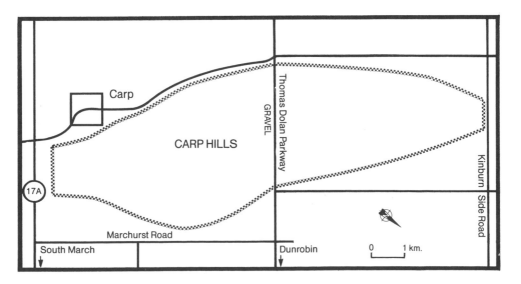

This area of Canadian Shield protrudes through the softer sedimentary rock in a broad band across West Carleton and Kanata. Its landscape offers great contrast with the surrounding area, being largely rolling, rugged bedrock knolls covered in sparse forest. Formerly zoned as conservation land by the Regional government, the Hills are now being developed in many places and the area's long term future is uncertain. For now, at least, it offers a delightfully wild island in the farmland of the Capital.

## Features:
Like a piece of Gatineau Park dropped into Ottawa-Carleton, the Carp Hills provide an area of Canadian Shield complete with a myriad of Beaver ponds, wet meadows, rock-knoll oak stands and young poplar - birch forests. A rich plant and animal life thrives on the Hills including many species seldom seen in the Capital south of the Ottawa River. The Beaver ponds offer nesting habitat for many ducks and other waterfowl (including a few Great Blue Herons) and are frequented by a small population of White-tailed Deer. A spectacular spring flora is exhibited in the South March Highlands (the southern extension of the Carp Hills), and includes a number of very unusual species. Similarly, breeding habitat for a number of rare birds, like the Blue-gray Gnatcatcher and Golden-winged Warbler, exists here. The northern section and the fringes of the southern section have proven to be important wintering habitat for raptors (including the spectacular Great Gray Owl) over a number of years.

## Visiting:
Access along the concession roads is good although it can be rough in winter. There are no formalized trails ; you must find your own way ... and that's half the fun of it. Favorite spots include side trips off the Thomas Dolan Parkway east of Carp, and north along the Goulbourn Forced Road west of Kanata. Driving the back roads in winter can turn up owls and other winter wildlife. Visitor facilities can be found in Carp and Kanata.

## Equipment and Considerations:
Binoculars are important here because the bird life is so rich. Most of the area is privately owned so you must respect posted lands and fences. Winter travel on the back roads should be undertaken with the possibility of getting stuck in mind. Sturdy footwear is important when hiking in this rugged landscape. Bring a map and compass (NTS map 31 F/8); you don't want to get lost while hiking across the hills.

## Seasonal Events & Considerations:
**Spring** - wildflower display, especially trilliums, along the Goulbourn Forced Road.
- night-time chorus of calling frogs and Woodcock throughout the Hills in April and May.
- woodland and wetland bird migration.

**Summer** - breeding birds in the rock knoll areas along the Thomas Dolan Parkway.
- rich flora of the hardwoods along the Goulbourn Forced Road and Old Carp Road.
- breeding waterfowl of the Beaver ponds.

**Fall** - fall colours along the Thomas Dolan Parkway.
- hawk migration along the edges of the Carp Hills.

Winter - wintering deer along the Huntley Townline Road.
- wintering raptors along the Marchhurst and Huntley Townline Roads.

**References:**

Brunton, D.F. 1981. South March Highlands : When is a Natural Environment Area NOT a Natural Environment Area? Trail & Landscape 15: 190-193.

Dore, W.G. 1968. Blue Phlox at its Northern Limit. Trail & Landscape 2: 71-75.

Kirwin, J.L. 1962. Geology of Part of the townships of March, Huntley and Nepean, Carleton County, Ontario. Canadian Field Naturalist 76: 108-115.

Solman, V.E.F. 1968. Explorer's Corner...A Spring Evening on Carp "Mountain". Trail & Landscape 2:40-41.

# 15) Shirleys Bay

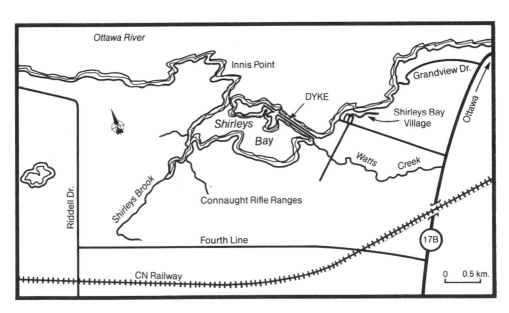

This quiet bay of the Ottawa River is situated partly in Nepean and partly in Kanata and is largely controlled by the federal government as an area for defence and astrophysical research and as a military base. As more and more of the Ottawa River shore is transformed from its natural state by development, this site's wildness enhances its environmental importance. Much of the area is off limits to the general public because of the sensi-tive activities being undertaken. Special arrangements can be made, however (see below) to permit visitors into this provincially significant natural area.

**Features:**
This is perhaps the best birdwatching spot in the Capital and one of the best in southern Ontario. That is the result of its geographic position on the important Ottawa River migration

route and the diversity of feeding and resting habitats offered to migrating birds. This is enhanced by the good water bird viewing opportunities from the earthen dyke that extends out from the mouth of Watts Creek to the islands in the bay. (That this dyke is a part of the sewage treatment program from the Region's Watts Creek plant is all too obvious to one's sense of smell on a warm day!). An extensive cat-tail marsh, maple swamp and array of upland forest types all contribute to the richness of Shirleys Bay for birding; about 270 species have been seen here over the years, mostly in the Watts Creek area and along the dyke. The Shirleys Bay area also supports some very unusual vegetation, the most important of these being the provincially significant alvar-shrub prairie at Innis Point. At this spot a number of northern and prairie species are found together in an attractive community that is a relict from ancient times. A large Wild Rice (*Zizania palustris*) stand thrives along Shirleys Brook, the small stream that enters the bay from the west and helps to freshen its polluted waters. The number of resting waterfowl at the mouth of this stream in the fall can be immense.

**Visiting:**
Arrangements for the use of particular sites within the Shirleys Bay area have been made by several organizations with the National Defence Department. You would be well advised to contact the Ottawa Field-Naturalists or the Ottawa Duck Club to find out about the limitations on their members' access and how you might be able to benefit from their arrangements. Public access is available at the boat launch at Shirleys Bay hamlet. The safety zone for the rifle ranges precludes access into the bay

from the water. Despite these difficulties, it is well worth finding a way to visit this fascinating area.

**Equipment and Considerations:**
Binoculars are essential in this birding area and a spotting telescope is virtually so if you wish to search the river and bay for waterfowl (including ducks, cormorants, grebes and geese) . Sturdy footwear and a good windbreaker are always advisable along the exposed dyke area. Poison-ivy is common in the scrubby woods along the river shore and is abundant in drier sites inland. Inland as well you may encounter the Prickly-ash, a low, painfully spiny shrub of open, calcareous sites ; it forms dense stands along the east side of Range Road.

**Seasonal Events & Suggestions:**
**Spring** - evening frog and Woodcock chorus in April and May along Range Road.
- waterfowl migration in the bay and at Watts Creek mouth in early spring.
- woodland bird migration in scrubby forest inland and in rivershore maple swamps.

**Summer** - rich flora in mature Silver Maple swamps at Innis Point and mouth of Watts Creek.
- seasonal flora on Innis Point alvar.

**Fall** - large numbers of migrating waterfowl in the bay, along the dyke and on the Ottawa River.
- large numbers of many species of shorebirds on mud flats at Watts Creek during low water periods.
- rich alvar vegetation at Innis Point.
- bird migration along the shoreline woodlands.
- migrating hawks over open fields inland and along the rivershore.

**References:**
Brunton, D.F. 1980. Shirleys Bay Life Sciences. Conservation Studies 1, National Capital Commission, Ottawa.

Gawn, S. 1979. Birding at Shirleys Bay. Trail & Landscape 13:170-173.

# 16) Stony Swamp Conservation Area

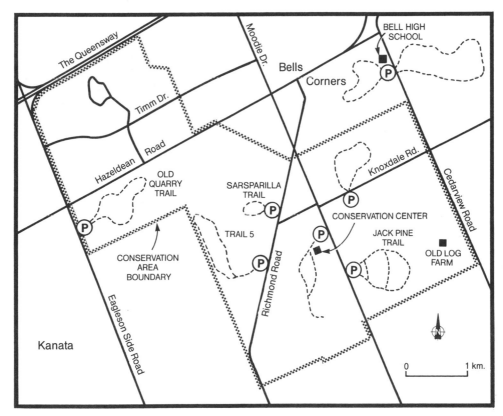

This almost 2000 hectares of woodland, wetland and overgrowing fields is situated in the expanding urban area of western Nepean. It is all federal government land, managed as a conservation area by the National Capital Commission. It is heavily used for recreational purposes by local residents as well as by visitors on a year-round basis. Despite its name, the area is only partly swamp land ; Stony Swamp Conservation Area is actually comprised of a variety of upland and lowland habitats which include examples of most typical natural situations found south of the Ottawa River.

**Features:**
The headwaters of several creeks as well as the Carp River originate in the swamp and marsh areas in the Moodie Drive - Richmond Road section of the conservation area. Since the bedrock consists of both limestone and sandstone (which is more acidic) a wide variety of plant species grow here. Indeed, over 700 species

are known from Stony Swamp - the largest total of any area in Canada's Capital. There are many interesting habitats. A fine Sugar Maple forest along the North-South Trail, small alvar clearings along Knoxdale Road, boggy wetlands west of Richmond Road under the power lines and regenerating pastures in a number of areas are just a few examples. An extensive network of trails provides year-round entry into most parts of the conservation area. An interpretive and environmental education program is conducted at the Interpretive Centre off Richmond Road and interpretive signs have been placed along the Sarsaparilla Trail just north of there. The Rideau Trail that runs from Ottawa to Kingston crosses the Stony Swamp. The large bird feeder operated on the Jack Pine Trail by the Ottawa Field Naturalists is usually a hive of activity, including bands of Black-capped Chickadees and even the occasional nuthatch that will land on your hand (or head !) in anticipation of an offering of sunflower seeds. Boardwalks take summer hikers across the beaver ponds on Jack Pine Trail and a number of the winter trails, though not officially maintained, are heavily used by hikers in the warm seasons too. The reptiles and amphibians of Stony Swamp are typical of those in most of the Capital, as are the breeding birds and mammals. The conservation area offers a cross-section of typical Capital area woodlands as well as many opportunities for visitors to get to know them.

**Visiting:**
Excellent access on a year-round basis is afforded by the surrounding road network. Toilet facilities are maintained in the summer at several trail heads and at the Interpretive Centre off Richmond Road. Parking lots are maintained at all trail heads. The Sarsaparilla Trail at Richmond Road is accessible by wheel-chair, as is the dock extending out onto the beaver pond off the trail. The others are less formally surfaced and require regular pedestrian abilities. Private transportation is necessary to reach many of the trail heads.

**Equipment and Considerations:**
Most trails have wet spots so waterproof boots are advisable in summer. The Jack Pine Trail and several others are so frequently travelled in winter that regular snow boots will suffice. Walking along ski trails should be avoided as this tends to damage the skiers' track. Binoculars are useful, especially in winter. A dip net for capturing aquatic life for (temporary) observation and identification is helpful. Mosquitoes can be fierce in swampy areas in late spring (such as along parts of the Sarsaparilla and Jack Pine Trails) and repellent is usually required. The Stony Swamp is very photogenic so bring along your camera at any season.

**Seasonal Events & Suggestions:**
**Spring** - woodland bird migration.
- wildflower display along Trail 5 and Jack Pine Trail.
- night-time frog chorus along Moodie Drive.

**Summer** - diverse flora throughout the area.
- beaver pond activity of Jack Pine Trail.
- breeding woodland birds along Trail 5 and Sarsaparilla Trail.
- wetland complex along Rideau Trail.

**Fall** - large numbers of Canada Geese and other waterfowl in fields along Cedarview Road.
- rich colour along Trails 5, 2 and 10.

152

- large numbers of ducks in ponds by the Old Log Farm and on the Sarsaparilla Trail.

**Winter** - tame chickadees and numerous other winter birds at feeder on the Jack Pine Trail.
- mammal track observation along all trails.
- Northern Flying Squirrels at Jack Pine Trail feeder at night.
- wintering birds in mixed and coniferous forest along Jack Pine Trail and Trail 5.

**References:**
Further information on interpretive programs in Stony Swamp Conservation Area can be obtained by contacting the interpretive staff at the National Capital Commission at 828-3620 (seasonally) or 827-2020.

Anonymous. (n.d.) The Greenbelt All Seasons Trail Map. National Capital Commission, Ottawa.

Brunton, D.F. 1982. Stony Swamp Life Sciences. Conservation Studies 5, National Capital Commission, Ottawa.

Gummer, Bill. 1984. What are those rocks we walk upon? Trail & Landscape 18: 181-185.

Peterkin, P. (Editor). 1981. Rideau Trail Notes. Rideau Trail Association, Ottawa.

# 17) Stillwater Creek

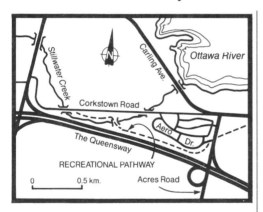

**Features:**
The valley of Stillwater Creek cuts deeply through thick marine clay, down to the sedimentary bedrock in some places. The steep slopes, heavy soil and extensive spring flooding have discouraged development along the creek. The Silver Maple forest in the creek bottom, as a consequence, is old and in good natural condition. An unusual addition is the abundance of Black Maple, a southern tree at the northern limit of its range in the Capital and seldom seen here in numbers. Near the pathway bridge there are some exceptionally large individual Black Maple trees. The eastern section of this area is a regenerating field; several exotic plants that spread from cultivation many years ago are common, including Bearded Iris *(Iris germanica)* and Thin-leaved Coneflower *(Rudbeckia triloba).* Rare native grasses and other woodland species are known from the creek banks.

Sandwiched between the Queensway on the south and Nepean subdivisions to the north and east, the Stillwater Creek section of the National Capital Commission's recreational pathway is easy to miss. It actually is an interesting strip of clay based, bottomland forest that contains a variety of pleasant surprises for the casual hiker who is interested in the natural world.

**Visiting:**
The recreational pathway from Acres Road to Moodie Drive offers excellent access to the creek bottom. You can enter through pedestrian gates at either road or through gates along Aero Drive. OC Transpo bus routes pass along Acres Road. There are no public facilities along the pathway.

**Equipment and Considerations:**
The gravel surface of the pathway requires no special footwear, though it can be flooded near the creek in spring. Binoculars will be an asset as bird life is very conspicuous along the trail. The clay soil become very slippery when wet; it is not wise to venture off the trail if rain has fallen recently.

**Seasonal Events and Suggestions:**
**Spring** - migrant woodland birds along the trail.

- ground flora along the creek banks.

**Summer** - large Black Maple trees along the path.
- common breeding birds of scrubby meadows conspicuous along trail.
- rich exotic flora, including unusual garden escapes.

**Fall** - migrant forest birds along the trail.
- spectacular Thin-leaved Coneflower display in early September.

**References:**
Dickson, H.L. 1980. Stillwater Creek. Trail & Landscape 14: 130-134.

Dickson, H.L. and S.J. Darbyshire. 1979. Biological Inventories of 24 Areas in the Ottawa District. Conservation Section, National Capital Commission, Ottawa.

# 18) Andrew Haydon Park (Ottawa Beach)

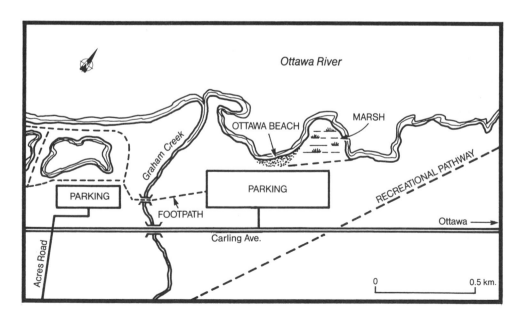

The eastern end of the city of Nepean's Andrew Haydon Park is an undeveloped open area overlooking the Ottawa River. Extensive mudflats form across the shallow bay each fall, providing important resting and feeding habitat for large numbers of waterfowl. They can sometime be seen here in the thousands. The shore and bay of the Ottawa Beach section (to use the names of the area before the park was built in the 1970's) were left in its present state at the urging of Ottawa naturalists when the rest of Graham Bay was obliterated by park development.

**Features:**
The bay off Ottawa Beach is very shallow and even in early summer provides a sand bar at the mouth of Graham Creek. By early fall when the Ottawa River water levels normally decline significantly, vast areas of sand and mud are exposed. Gulls, geese, ducks and herons rest here in large numbers and shorebirds (sandpipers, plovers, yellowlegs, etc.) feed on the invertebrates at or near the surface. By late fall hundreds - or even thousands - of Canada Geese are present in the offshore shallows. They are frequently accompanied by a number of other waterfowl species. Raptors, including the rare Peregrine Falcon, can also be seen as they hunt for weak or injured waterfowl. Many records of species new to the Capital or rare here, including the first record for Ontario of the Lesser Black-backed Gull, have been made between Ottawa Beach and the Britannia Pier. The mudflats also support unusual plant life, although these are being reduced by the ever increasing numbers of Purple Loosestrife. That tall, beautiful plant is a recent arrival in the Capital but is all too successful, choking out native wetland vegetation as it multiplies.

**Visiting:**
The parking area off Carling Avenue is accessible from the spring to the fall. The recreational pathways through Haydon Park and along the old railway right-of-way to the east also provide access and observation points. A car provides an effective blind from which to observe the waterfowl when they are close to the shore ; in this way you stay dry and comfortable even in nasty weather and the birds are not bothered. This vehicular access makes it a good site for disabled observers to watch waterfowl.

**Equipment and Considerations:**
Binoculars are essential for a good view of the waterfowl ; a telescope is even better, especially if you wish to scan the waters of Lake Deschenes for diving ducks and other distant birds. The site can be muddy so rain boots are advisable. There are no facilities here but washrooms, picnic tables and even a dynamite 'big toy' play structure for small children can all be found in the developed part of Andrew Haydon Park. That area is connected with the waterfowl beach by a walking/bicycle path. You should always remember that the animals you are watching are engaged in a demanding and dangerous task, the challenge of migrating across thousands of kilometers of unknown territory. They need the rest, security and nourishment that their brief stay at Ottawa Beach provides. PLEASE do not disturb them.

**Seasonal Events & Suggestions:**
**Summer-** migrating shorebirds on the mudflats from late July.
- roosting gulls on the sand spit at Graham Creek in the evening.

155

**Fall** - continuing shorebird migration, peaking in late August and early September.
- huge numbers of resting gulls on the shore, in the shallows and along the edge of the ice until freeze-up.
- huge numbers of Canada Geese resting in the shallows with many ducks, from September until late November.
- unusual mudflat flora off the main beach and eastward to the Britannia Pier.

**References:**
Dickson, H.L. 1981. Ottawa Beach. Trail & Landscape 15: 13-15.

# 19) Britannia Conservation Area

This is a level, wooded area centered on Mud Lake, a former embayment of the Ottawa River. It is surrounded by urban development on all sides, yet retains a delightfully wild character that is highly appreciated by the residents of Britannia. Indeed, when plans to destroy this site to make way for another bridge across the river were announced in the early 1970's, the outcry from the adjacent community did not stop until the project was shelved. Local residents remain vigilant lest this National Capital Commission conservation area be threatened again. The woods are heavily used by recreationalists and naturalists alike.

**Features:**
Britannia contains examples of many habitats. A White Pine stand on the west side of the lake is beautiful year-round (though especially in winter) and often shelters wintering Porcupines and/or Great Horned Owls. The small oak-maple woods to the north of the pinery is attractive too when the flush of spring wildflowers arrives. Small migrating birds are common in the tangle of shrubbery between the wildflowers and Cassels Road in the spring and fall. Britannia Woods is one of the best bird watching sites in the Capital; Over 200 species have been recorded here, some of which are extremely rare. At the south end of Mud Lake is a large Buttonbush swamp (itself an unusual feature) where large numbers of ducks can be seen each fall. The swamp forest also contains many Painted Turtles and even a few of the uncommon Blanding's Turtles. Several active Beaver lodges are situated in Mud Lake and the Beaver can often be seen swimming to and from them. Add to all this a rich and diverse flora that includes a large number of rare species and you can appreciate why the Britannia Conservation Area is considered to be one of the top ten natural areas on federal land in Canada's Capital.

**Visiting:**
Year-round access is easy; an informal series of paths covers much of the area, originating from a number of pedestrian gates through the boundary fence. Parking is available along side streets and at the Britannia Filtration Plant. There are no facilities in the area and access for the disabled is difficult. OC Transpo bus routes run along Britannia Road and a recreational pathway is maintained in the summer along the southern boundary of the woods.

**Equipment and Considerations:**
Normal seasonal clothing will suffice. Mosquitoes can be bad, especially near the Buttonbush swamp, early in the summer. Much of the woods is Poison-ivy heaven and you should be careful and alert to this when leaving the relative safety of the trails. An uncommon shrub, Prickly-ash, is locally abundant south of Mud Lake and is painfully thorny. Stick to the trails, however, and the Prickly-ash won't stick to you. Binoculars are important for observing migrating forest birds and the mammals (Porcupines, Snowshoe Hare, Cottontail Rabbit, etc.) that occupy the woods. If you wish to get a better look at the turtles or want to search for salamanders along the lake edge, rubber boots are advised.

**Seasonal Events & Suggestions:**
**Spring** - observing diving ducks and gulls off the Filtration Plant at the river in April and May.
- small forest bird migration (especially on rainy days) in late April to mid-May.
- spring wildflowers in the maple-oak woods and along the south side of Mud Lake.
- swallows and Purple Martins feeding over the fields and water areas.
Summer - large colony of Cliff Swallows nesting on the filtration plant building with the more common Barn Swallows.
- turtles sunning on logs in Mud Lake and the Buttonbush swamp.
- world's smallest plant, Water-meal *(Wolffia spp.),* abundant along the edge of the Buttonbush swamp.
- rich bird song along the recreational pathway at dusk.
- exotic flora at woodland edges and along the ridge on Cassels Road, including a Red Mulberry tree by the Cassels Road gate.

**Fall** - bird migration in the woods, on the river off the Filtration Plant and along the Cassels Road ridge.
- numbers of ducks, including the spectacular Wood Duck, in the Buttonbush swamp.
- Beaver adding to their winter food supply by lodges on the lake and along the outlet stream.

**Winter** - wintering small birds (finches, woodpeckers, etc.) in the woods.
- Great Horned Owls and Porcupine occasionally in the White Pine stand.
- scenic beauty of the pond and pines after a snowfall.
- large population of golden-eye, mergansers and other ducks wintering in the Deschenes Rapids and along the Cassels Road channel.

**References:**
Billington, C. and E.W. Tozer. 1977. Ecological Inventory of NCC Urban Areas. Interpretation Section, National Capital Commission, Ottawa.

Brunton, D.F. 1979. Explorer's Corner...Britannia. Trail & Landscape 3: 28-29.

Brunton, D.F. 1984. Nature Reserve

Potential and Management in the National Capital Region on National Capital Commission Lands, Ontario/Quebec. Conservation Studies 29, National Capital Commission, Ottawa.

# 20) Pinhey Forest Reserve

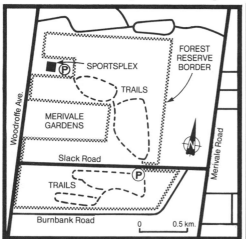

The area behind the Nepean Sportsplex between Woodroffe Avenue and Merivale Road is managed as a forest reserve by the National Capital Commission. It supports a complex of different woodlands growing on sand laid down during post-glacial events. Scrubby fields indicate the degree of disturbance but offer easy travel with a wide variety of natural features to be seen.

## Features:
In old post-glacial sand dunes that have been long stabilized by tree cover acidic, bog-like sloughs support a variety of northern plants in what is otherwise a fairly typical Silver Maple swamp. The dunes were planted with poplar and Red Pine many years ago, resulting in a loss of much of their natural value. Along the north side of Slack Road however, a low Red Maple forest supports a rich ground flora in the spring and a number of un-

usual plants through the summer. The coniferous and mixed forests offer shelter for many wintering birds, including Ruffed Grouse and owls. The summer vegetation here is very different from that of the Red Maple forest. The scrubby field area beyond these woods contains a number of interesting non-native species of plants - a record of the history of human activity there. Being the only large area of woodland in the immediate vicinity, the Pinhey Forest Reserve offers good shelter for many winter wildlife species.

## Visiting:
The city of Nepean and the National Capital Commission maintain a complex of summer and winter trails in the forest reserve. They offer access into the whole area. The Fitness Trail behind the Sportsplex is accessible to disabled persons. Hiking in the area is generally easy, on dry, relatively open, level ground. OC Transpo bus routes run along the south and west side of the area. There are toilets and picnic tables by the trail parking are on the south side of Slack Road and an abundance of parking behind the Sportsplex (year-round).

## Equipment and Considerations:
Regular outdoor footwear is sufficient in summer. Biting insects can be fierce in early summer, especially in the slough area along Slack Road. This is a good spot for general landscape photography.

**Seasonal Events & Suggestions:**
**Spring** - wildflowers in the Red Maple forest along Slack Road.
- migrant woodland birds behind the Sportsplex.

**Summer** - uncommon plants of boggy sloughs, including Labrador Tea, off Slack Road Trail (Number 2).
- interesting non-native flora in weedy fields east of the Sportsplex.

**Winter** - wintering birds in the conifers along Slack Road and behind the Sportsplex.

**References:**
Brunton, D.F. 1984. Nature Reserve Potential and Management in the National Capital Region on National Capital Commission Lands, Ontario/Quebec. Conservation Studies 29, National Capital Commission, Ottawa.

Mosquin, T. and J.M. Gillett. 1984. Inventory and Evaluation of Vegetation of the Pinhey Forest Reserve. Conservation Studies 33, National Capital Commission, Ottawa.

# 21) Carlington Woods

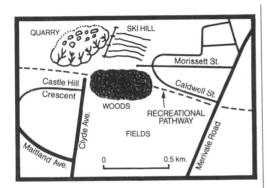

This small area perched atop a limestone bluff provides a panoramic view of most of the west end of Ottawa and the Gatineau Hills. It is maintained by the National Capital Commission and is surrounded by residential and industrial development. The small woodland contains several interesting natural features and offers Carlington residents a pleasant, reasonably natural landscape.

**Features:**
The woodland is dominated by young maple, oak, hickory and Basswood ; scattered clumps of Eastern Hemlock and White Cedar are found in wet spots. Limestone bedrock outcrops frequently. Scrubby fields extend southward from the woods, dominated by non-native plant species. The woodland edge is a favoured feeding area for several uncommon wintering birds. Such rare winter species as American Robin, Saw-whet Owl and even Mockingbird have been seen repeatedly. The small black berries that are abundant on the Common Buckthorn (*Rhamnus cathartica*) here appear to be a major winter food source for many of these birds. Being a small woodlot in a built-up section of the city makes this a good migrant trap; birds landing anywhere in the vicinity will head straight for the natural forest cover. Some exceptional sightings have resulted. By midsummer the weed species in the fields to the south are a delightful, colourful spectacle, especially the Brown Knapweed (*Centaurea jacea*) that is present in the thousands.

**Visiting:**
Park at the top of the reservoir at the west end of Morisset Drive and walk in along the recreational pathway that crosses the woods. There are a num-

ber of informal, rough trails running through the woods in several places. Only the surfaced bike path would be suitable for disabled visitors. There are no facilities here.

## Equipment and Considerations:
Binoculars and a camera are useful in light of the rich bird life and the panoramic view of the surrounding landscape. Sturdy footwear in advisable if venturing off the paved path. Poison-ivy is common and some of the dense clumps of hawthorn can cause painful scratches for those exploring the woods and not being attentive to their surroundings. Keep children in hand if going anywhere near the very deep quarry to the northwest of the woods; a fall would almost certainly be fatal.

## Seasonal Events & Suggestions:
**Spring** - migrant birds in the woods (May).

**Summer** - weedy vegetation in the south fields.

**Fall** - migrant forest birds in the woods; migrant raptors in the south fields.

**Winter** - wintering birds sheltering in the woods; Bohemian Waxwings feeding on buckthorn fruit in late winter.

## References:
Brunton, D.F. 1984. Nature Reserve Potential & Management in the National Capital Region on National Capital Commission Lands, Ontario/Quebec. Conservation Studies 29, National Capital Commission, Ottawa.

# 22) Central Experimental Farm

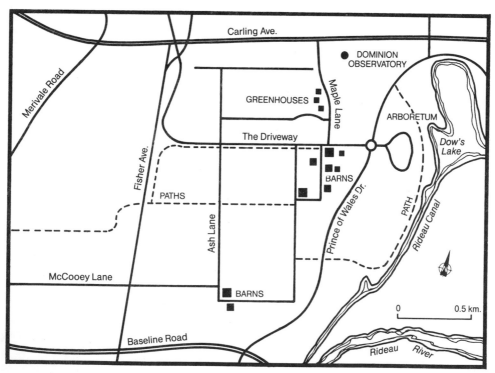

What a remarkable feature it is, a huge area of farmland, complete with buildings, livestock and the appropriate sounds and smells, extending from Dows Lake all the way to Merivale Road. This pastoral landscape of rolling, deep-soiled agricultural fields and research facilities has been a feature of the Ottawa area for over a century. Not only does it provide important agricultural research but its quiet, green presence calms our collective spirit and helps to clean the air we breathe as well as being a surprisingly large attraction to a great many wildlife species.

**Features:**
Much of the attraction for wildlife on the Farm results from deliberate attempts to change the landscape. The Arboretum near Dows Lake is an example. The large variety of trees there offers a heavy bounty of fruit and seed for wintering birds as well as opportunities for shelter and nesting. Many rare species have been seen here over the years. The exotic trees are of interest in themselves, demonstrating the colour and form of species from around the world and how such plants can grow surprisingly well in Ottawa's climate. Open country birds can be found in the fields west of the main barns; Gray Partridge, a delightful introduction that is resident in eastern Ontario, is found in the fall and winter by the manure piles at the cattle barns and in the fields. With the first warm days of late February Horned Larks are found singing beautifully over these fields, each male furiously proclaiming the arrival of spring from his own fence post. Rock Doves and House Sparrows are year-round residents about the buildings where they can benefit from the seed spilled from live-stock feeding operations. In many years, one or more Snowy Owls can be seen on the fields in winter. Gulls and even shorebirds use these same fields in fall for resting and feeding during migration. The ornamental Macoun Gardens by the traffic circle are attractive to more than wedding parties and envious gardeners; flower-loving birds like the Ruby-throated Hummingbird are resident in summer. Other birds frequent the garden to feed on the insect life attracted by the magnificent floral display. When the farm supported more wild sections than it does now it was considered a national wildlife sanctuary. While no longer offering wildness, it still provides a pleasant and at times very productive area for urban naturalists.

**Visiting:**
Year-round access by car and on foot is excellent and the Farm also offers fine summer biking. Public washroom facilities are available in a number of Agriculture Canada buildings (e.g. by the Agricultural Museum) throughout the year. In summer, horse drawn carts take visitors on tours of the Farm grounds. OC Transpo bus routes run along Prince of Wales Drive (Highway 16) and on other major peripheral roads.

**Equipment and Considerations:**
No particular precautions are required. Binoculars and a camera are useful in documenting a visit to this delightful place.

**Seasonal Events & Suggestions:**
**Spring** - migrating field birds along southern Ash and McCooey Lanes.
- small woodland birds in migration at the Arboretum in May.

**Summer** - common field birds of Capital farm lands (Eastern Meadowlark,

Savannah Sparrow, etc.) in the fields.

**Fall** - shorebirds (especially Black-bellied and Golden Plovers) in the recently tilled fields in late August and September.
- gulls following tractors plowing fields.

**Winter** - Gray Partridge along fence rows and at manure piles.
- Bohemian Waxwings (most years) and other unusual winter birds feeding on fruit trees in the Arboretum.
- Snowy Owls along McCooey Lane, hunting from fenceposts.
- Evening (and often Pine) Grosbeaks feeding on ash seeds along Ash Lane and on fruit in the Arboretum.

**References:**
Anstey, T.H. 1986. One Hundred Harvests. Historical Series 27, Research Branch, Agriculture Canada, Ottawa.

DeLury, R.E. 1925. The Experimental Farm as a Bird Sanctuary. Canadian Field-Naturalist 39: 1-4.

# 23) The Marlborough Forest

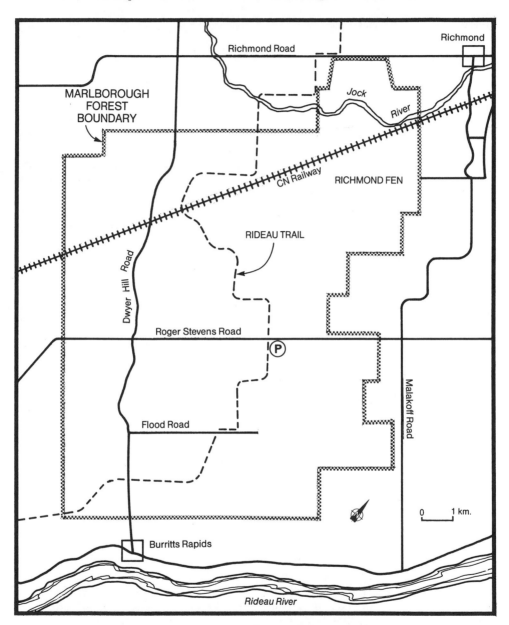

Roger Stevens Drive west of North Gower cuts across the middle of the vast Marlborough Forest, an area of public and private land that supports a diversity of habitats. The topog- raphy is relatively level. Over 6500 hectares are owned by the Regional Municipality of Ottawa-Carleton and managed as conservation land by the Ontario Ministry of Natural Resources.

This is the largest conservation area in Ottawa-Carleton and despite many private land holdings offers excellent ground for exploration and discovery by hikers and naturalists alike.

### Features:

This is an area of extensive wetlands, with upland forests intervening. Fens, swamps, marshes and Beaver ponds occur throughout, with forests of hardwoods, mixed hardwood - coniferous and White Cedar stands occupying upland sites in thin soil. Limestone bedrock underlies the whole area. Small alvar clearings are found throughout the southern portion of the Forest, especially in the southwest corner. The wetlands are probably of most interest to the naturalist, however. The Richmond Fen, a large calcareous wetland south of Richmond, is best known for its small population of elusive and secretive Yellow Rails, and for stands of the Prairie Fringed-orchid *(Platanthera leucophaea)* which is rare in Canada. It is a permanently flooded, open grassy area that has probably looked much like this for thousands of years. Its cool microclimate has encouraged a flora and fauna to develop that is more typical of northern areas. Typically northern birds like Sedge and Winter Wren, Olive-sided and Yellow-bellied Flycatcher, Golden-crowned Kinglet and Yellow Rail have been known to nest here or in the adjacent coniferous forest. The butterflies of the site, like the plant species, exhibit this northern affinity. Another fen just south of here, the Phragmites Fen, is different in form but has a similar plant and insect life to the Richmond Fen. The long, narrow shape of the Phragmites Fen has less habitat for northern birds.

### Visiting:

A private vehicle is necessary for access to the out-of-the-way corners of the Forest but even this won't get you to some of the wetlands. The excellent map prepared by the Regional Municipality of Ottawa-Carleton (see references, below) is required if you want to know all of your trail options. You should also consider checking with local naturalists' clubs or the Rideau Trail Association to see if they have any outings scheduled into the more hard-to-reach areas. A good cross-section of the forest can be seen along the Rideau Trail which runs right across the Forest in a north-south direction. Skiing and snowmobile trails are also available.

### Equipment and Considerations:

A picnic area, with parking and toilet facilities, is maintained on Roger Stevens Drive where the Rideau Trail crosses. Camping is not permitted here but hunting is, so be careful in the fall when walking the trails. The dry, open woodland edges throughout the Forest are ideal for Poison-ivy and it is very common. Mosquitoes can be bad in early summer especially in the fens where their numbers take on legendary proportions ! Good footwear, a willingness to get dirty and the ability to put out a good deal of effort is required of anyone wishing to visit the fen areas. Upland sites are much easier going, but be prepared for considerable midday heat of the rock flats in summer. A small pack containing food, drink and an emergency kit, is always a good idea for a back-country trip.

### Seasonal Events & Suggestions:

**Spring** - early flowering plants, including violets and orchids, in the fens.
- migrant woodland birds along the wetland periphery.

- wildflower display in clearings in the White Cedar woods and in hardwoods.

**Summer** - breeding northern birds, including rare species, in the Richmond Fen.
- rare flora of the fens and alvar clearings.
- evening chorus of frogs and night birds (including Whip-poor-wills) along the wetland periphery.

**Fall** - migrating birds through woodland and open meadows.
- rich alvar flora along east end of Flood Road.

**References:**
Peterkin, P. 1981. (Editor) . Rideau Trail Notes. Rideau Trail Association, Ottawa.

Planning Department. 1985. Marlborough Forest Information Map. Regional Municipality of Ottawa-Carleton, Ottawa.

Reddoch, J. 1979. Calcareous Fens in the Ottawa District. Trail & Landscape 13: 16-27.

Reddoch, J., *et al.* 1977. Ottawa-Carleton Regional Forest. Trail & Landscape 11: 6-21.

White, D.J. 1985. A Life Science Inventory of Parts of the Marlborough Regional Forest. Parks Branch, Ministry of Natural Resources, Kemptville (Unpublished Report).

# 24) Baxter Conservation Area

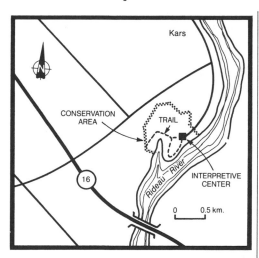

At a curve in the Rideau River about 8 km southeast of North Gower, the Baxter Conservation Area occupies almost 70 hectares of floodplain in Rideau Township. It offers a pleasant day trip south of Ottawa while giving visitors the opportunity of exploring river shore swamp forest.

**Features:**
Centuries of deposition of fine silt and sand by the spring flooding Rideau River has resulted in the low, moist situation here. A fine old Red Maple swamp dominates the area west of the Interpretive Centre and visitors can easily enter this cool, lush-green, shady forest. The undergrowth is characterized by flood tolerant plant species, including many ferns. A number of significant plants, including two provincially rare species, occur here. Immediately west of the maple swamp is a cat-tail marsh. A foot bridge crosses the marsh and leads to a White Cedar bush (and a planted Black Walnut grove) on the far side. As Baxter Conservation Area is situated along a flyway for migratory birds, the rush of warblers and other

small woodland species in the spring can be impressive. The low, wet conditions are excellent for a variety of amphibians and reptiles.

## Visiting:

The area is open year-round, with washrooms, picnic tables and a swimming beach available in summer. A ski trail is marked out in winter. Parking is available by the Interpretive Centre, where environmental education programs for school children are run throughout the year. The Fiddlehead Trail follows a looped path that starts and ends at the Centre ; it has slightly different routes in summer and winter. Interpretive brochures for this self-guiding trail are available at the trail head for both the summer and winter versions. Signs along Highway 16 near the North Gower turn off direct travellers eastward to Baxter Conservation Area.

## Equipment and Considerations:

Although the trails are surprisingly dry in mid-summer, they can be awash in the spring. You should wear rubber boots and be prepared for lots of mosquitoes in the late spring and early summer. The Fiddlehead Trail is wide and easy to follow, though not recommended for disabled persons because of the unevenness of the surface and occasional low spots. Binoculars are useful but the woods are too dark for most photographic purposes.

## Seasonal Events & Considerations:

**Spring** - salamanders active in the flooded maple forest.
- evening chorus of frogs (Spring Peepers, Wood Frogs, Striped Chorus Frog) in April.
- migrating woodland birds in May.
- flowering of the Red Maples and Silver Maples in early May.
**Summer** - rich undergrowth of ferns in the maple swamp.
- breeding rivershore birds in alder thickets.
- common marsh birds and basking turtles in the marsh west of Fiddlehead Trail.

**Winter** - Snowshoe Hares in underbrush along Fiddlehead Trail.
- common winter woodland birds at feeders at Interpretive Centre and along trail.

## References:

Further information on public facilities and the environmental education program can be obtained by calling the Rideau Valley Conservation Authority at 692-3571 or the Baxter Conservation Area at 489-3592.

# 25) Rockcliffe Park

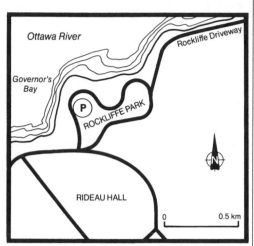

The park is situated along the Ottawa River along the west side of the village of Rockcliffe and just east of the Governor-General's residence in eastern Ottawa. Although the parkway, bandshells, manicured lawns and lookouts give it a civilized appearance, it holds real interest to the naturalist in a number of places along the river shore.

## Features:

Along the steep river bank (especially in Governor's Bay) natural oak, elm, ash and Sugar Maple forest persists. It grows in thin, dry soil over limestone bedrock and includes a small stand of Hackberry and clumps of White Cedar. Some unusual exotic species have become established in clearings and along the edge of these woods. Where the limestone bedrock forms steep rock faces, uncommon ferns can be found. Salamanders scurry about the shattered bedrock talus below. The wooded shoreline offers resting and feeding habitat for migrating birds; several extremely rare species have been observed here.

## Visiting:

Access from the Rockcliffe Driveway is good year-round. Parking lots are maintained at several locations and a variety of formal and informal trails run throughout the area.

## Equipment and Considerations:

Binoculars are necessary for observing birds out on the river. Sturdy footgear is advisable when venturing on the informal trails and along the shore of the river. Be careful near the river shore ; the cliffs along sections of Governor's Bay are painfully high and the rock at the top is not stable.

## Seasonal Events & Suggestions:

**Summer** - uncommon plants along the shore slopes at Governor's Bay.
- Red-backed Salamanders (lead-backed phase) along the shore.
- common breeding woodland birds.

## References:

Darbyshire, S.J. 1982. Rockcliffe Park. Trail & Landscape 16: 66-68.

Dickson, H.L. and S.J. Darbyshire. 1979. Biological Inventory of 23 Areas in the Ottawa Region, Conservation Section, National Capital Commission, Ottawa.

# 26) Green's Creek Conservation Area

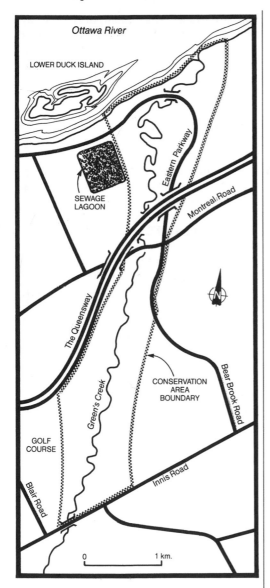

This conservation area occupies about 400 hectares of hilly land in Gloucester west of Orleans, between the Ottawa River and Innes Road along Green's Creek. It is situated in heavy marine clay and shows many examples of landslides and slumping of this unstable material. The deeply cut valley of Green's Creek and its clay substrate have discouraged development. While this also makes access more difficult, it has helped to maintain relatively natural sections of forest land along the creek. The conservation area is managed by the National Capital Commission as part of the Greenbelt.

**Features:**
As the clay slopes erode along the creek and at its mouth at the Ottawa River, hard, rock-like nodules of clay are exposed. For over a century scientists have been breaking open these nodules because some, for as yet undetermined reasons, contain fossils of plants and animals that date from the Champlain Sea period about 10,000 years ago. This important geological phenomenon is considered to be of national significance. So too are some of the plants that grow in the Silver Maple swamps along the creek, including Ontario's largest stand of rare Cat-tail Sedge (Carex typhina). Witchhazel, a southern shrub found nowhere else in the Regional Municipality of Ottawa-Carleton, occurs in large numbers in the rich, well drained hardwood forest above the river mouth. Further upstream rich Eastern Hemlock forests dominate ravine vegetation along tributaries. In one of these a stand of the rare Pinedrops (Pterospora andromedea) is found; it is one of the small number of plants that must get nutrients from other plants, being unable to manufacture their own. It grows with an uncommon Rattlesnake-plantain Orchid, (Goodyera tesselata), another of these unusual saprophytic plants. In

the largest part, however, the Green's Creek Conservation Area exhibits typical flora and fauna of the clay based areas of Gloucester and offers visitors a good opportunity to get to know many of them.

## Visiting:

Access is good along the recreational pathway by the Eastern Driveway, where the Silver Maple swamps can be reached. Ravine forests can be entered most easily from the northwest corner of the National Capital Commission nursery off Innes Road or from the northeast corner of the Pineview Golf Course off Blair Road. Travel is rugged, requiring bushwacking and negotiating of steep slopes throughout. Cross-country skiing along the creek in winter is somewhat simpler. There are no public facilities in the area. OC Transpo bus routes use major roads around the conservation area.

## Equipment and Considerations:

A sturdy pair of boots is important here. Do not enter the area in wet weather or just after a rainfall ; the clay become unbelievably slippery and dangerous (to say nothing of messy) to walk on. The steep slopes frequently experience landslides in spring, so you should avoid all open slopes that appear weak or have cracks visible on the surface. Binoculars are useful for observing the bird life along the creek .

## Seasonal Events & Suggestions:

**Spring** - bird migration along the Green's Creek and at the creek mouth.
- wildflowers in the ravine and hardwood forests.

**Summer** - unusual ravine vegetation near Innes Road.
- clay nodules eroding from banks along Green's Creek.**

**Fall**- rich Silver Maple swamp flora near Ottawa River.
- flowering Witch-hazel shrubs along the recreational pathway at the creek mouth in September and October.

**Winter** - northern finches and owls wintering in conifer stands along the creek.

## References:

Brunton, D.F. 1983. An Ecological Inventory of the Green's Creek Sector, National Capital Commission Greenbelt, Gloucester, Ontario. Conservation Studies 15, National Capital Commission, Ottawa.

Darbyshire, S.J. and H.L. Dickson. 1980. Witch Hazel in the Ottawa Area. Trail & Landscape 14: I58-160.

Harington, C.R. 1983. Significance of the Fossil Locality at Green's Creek, Ontario. Trail & Landscape 17: 164-178.

*\*\* These nodules are important geological resources and should not be taken as souvenirs. It is also an offense under the National Capital Act to remove any from National Capital Commission lands.*

# 27) Lower Duck Island

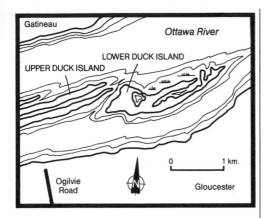

Situated just downstream of Upper Duck Island in the Ottawa River is Gloucester's Lower Duck Island. It is the result of centuries of accumulated sand deposition by the currents of the Ottawa River. It is essentially untouched ... a real gem of a natural area. This National Capital Commission area is considered ecologically to be of provincial significance.

**Features:**
The wet swamp forests on the lowest areas of the island are dominated by mature Silver Maple under which large beds of Ostrich Fern have developed. This grades into marsh and aquatic vegetation of considerable richness and diversity, especially on the north side of the island.It also supports healthy populations of various species of common frogs and turtles. A mature Hackberry forest on the drier, higher ground on the west end of the island is an exceptional example of rich southern hardwoods and supports a number of unusual southern plants. The forests of Lower Duck Island have probably been precisely in this condition for centuries, with new trees replacing older ones removed by windthrow, lightning, erosion and other natural disturbances. The isolation of the island has protected it from development and allows us to see one of the few Ottawa River islands that remain in a natural state.

**Visiting:**
A boat is required for summer access; you can launch from either the Eastern Driveway near Green's Creek (Gloucester) or from Hurtubise Boulevard (Gatineau). There are no facilities on the island.

**Equipment and Considerations:**
The undergrowth can be a tangle in places so you should be prepared for some thrashing about on the edges of the island ; the mature forests offer easier going. There is lots of Poison-ivy here, so be prepared. Take a camera along; you may not have a chance to visit such rich woodlands again for a long, long time.

**Seasonal Events & Suggestions:**
**Summer**- rich flora of the Hackberry stand at the west end.
- diverse aquatic flora on the island margins.
- reptiles and amphibian populations around the island.

**Fall**- unusual flora of upland forest area.
- rich colour of the changing hardwoods.

**References:**
Brunton, D.F. 1984. Nature Reserve Potential and Management on National Capital Commission Lands in the National Capital Region, Ontario/Quebec. Conservation Studies

29, National Capital Commission, Ottawa.

Darbyshire, S.J. 1981. Upper Duck and Lower Duck Islands. Trail & Landscape 15: 133-140.

Dickson, H.L. and S.J. Darbyshire. 1979. Biological Inventory of 23 Areas in the Ottawa Region. Conservation Section, National Capital Commission, Ottawa.

# 28) Mer Bleue Conservation Area

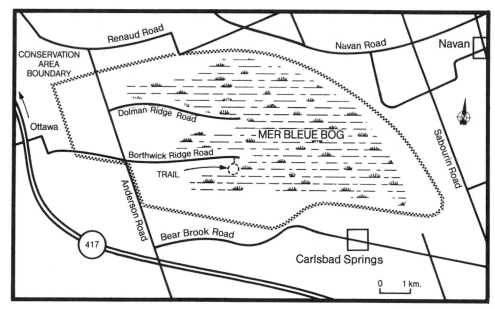

The Mer Bleue bog is the focal point of natural lands in this area. It is a huge peatland of almost 5000 hectares, 3100 of which are owned by the National Capital Commission and managed as conservation lands. When the land in the Capital was recovering from the weight of thousands of years (and hundreds of meters) of glacial ice, various drainage channels formed, changed and disappeared. One such channel formed a large depression east of Ottawa. When it ceased to function about 9000 years ago, a huge wetland was left on poorly drained clay and it became the Mer Bleue. This immense bog is one of the largest in southern Ontario and is perhaps the most important natural area in the Regional Municipality of Ottawa-Carleton. Ecologically it is considered to be of provincial or national significance and has been the object of biological study for over a century.

**Features:**
The most striking natural feature of the area is the bog mat itself, a "sea" of deep, saturated peat overtopped by open heath and stunted to moderate-sized Black Spruce and Tamarack forest. The mat is home to a variety of plants, some rare, some common and almost all exhibiting unusual characteristics enabling them to

survive in this demanding environment. Some literally eat insects, some have features of desert plants and others rarely rely on seeds for reproduction. These include the Pitcher-plant *(Sarracenia purpurea)*, some rare orchids, several species of cotton-grass *(Eriophorum spp.)* and a variety of low heath shrubs. This habitat is ecologically a piece of northern Ontario wetland and has not changed a great deal in thousands of years. It is home for a variety of exceptional animals too, including the nationally rare Spotted Turtle and Fletcher's Dragonfly, an insect known from only a handful of sites worldwide. The richest part of the bog is The Islands - small sand outcrops (old sand bars) in the middle of the bog. They are covered by poplar and birch and are found where the bog mat is youngest, wettest and richest. A moat surrounds the mat. For millennia, Beaver have flooded the streams flowing out of the bog, creating a marshy/swampy wetland. The lagg, as it is technically known, is a marvellous place for turtles and frogs, as well as common swamp birds such as Alder Flycatcher, Swamp Sparrow, Northern Yellowthroat and Common Grackle.

A large cat-tail area, Ramsayville Marsh, has developed along Anderson Road by the Canadian National Railway track and contains an assortment of typical marsh birds. It is becoming very ingrown, however, and now supports fewer species of waterfowl than it did some years ago. Without the influence of fire or an equivalent natural disturbance, Ramsayville Marsh will become less important for wildlife as the cat-tail becomes completely dominant. The upland areas of the Mer Bleue Conservation Area are of considerable biological interest too. The Ridges, as they are known, are huge sand bars and islands that formed in the postglacial drainage channel. They now support extensive hardwood, coniferous and mixed forests as well as large regenerating pasture areas. Some of the Ridge plants are relicts of the time when these were scrubby knolls in a cold, boreal landscape. Old Red Maple forests on the lower slopes of the Ridges contain lush fern undergrowth as well as provincially rare plants such as the Large Purple-fringed Orchid *(Platanthera grandiflora).* These upland habitats combine with the wetland environment to offer the Capital a unique complex of natural diversity.

**Visiting:**
The Ridges are easily reached along major routes like Dolman, Borthwick and Anderson Roads. They can be explored on the network of walking and ski trails maintained by the National Capital Commission. Toilet facilities are available at several of these trail heads and parking is ample. A private vehicle is necessary for getting to the trails. The bog mat is another question, however, because of the lagg surrounding it and due to concern for its protection. The short answer is DON'T go onto it. There is a self-guiding boardwalk trail off the Borthwick Ridge that will take visitors out onto the bog mat without causing damage to the delicate vegetation ... or the visitors! Ramsayville Marsh can be observed best along the drainage channels crossing Anderson Road ; be cautious on the narrow road shoulder when pulling off here.

**Equipment and Considerations:**
Regular walking shoes should suffice for most of the trails, although wet and rough spots can be found on many. Mosquitoes can be very bad in early summer and deer flies are mur-

172

der on hot days in mid-summer (wear a hat). Binoculars are a great help in scanning across the bog and ridges. A camera would be used frequently too. DO NOT venture out on the bog alone. It is dirty, very hard going and potentially quite dangerous, to say nothing of damaging to the mat. Contact the Conservation Section of the National Capital Commission to see what arrangements can be made for a small group trip (if any). The area around the islands may still have unexploded bombs from the practice bombing that was conducted there several decades ago by the air force, although such duds (the bombs, that is) are likely buried deeply in the peat.

**Seasonal Events & Suggestion:**
**Spring** - marsh birds at Ramsayville Marsh.
- Cottongrass in abundant flower on the bog mat.
- wildflowers on Dolman Ridge (west) trails.

**Summer** - rich flora and breeding birds of Red Maple forests along the Ridges.
- bog mat vegetation along the boardwalk trail on Borthwick Ridge (east end).
- unusual turtles (Blanding's and Spotted) in the lagg pools.
- non-native plants of regenerating old pastures on the Ridges.
- rich flora of young Ridge hardwoods.

**Fall** - migrating marshbirds, including thousands of Red-winged Blackbirds and Common Grackles, in Ramsayville Marsh.
- changing vegetation colour in scrub forest and young hardwoods on the Ridges.

**Winter** - mammal tracks throughout the bog, including those of Otter, Marten, Coyote and Red Squirrel.
- skiing trip out to the Islands from the Ridges.
- winter birds in coniferous woods along the bog margin.

**References:**
You should contact the National Capital Commission (Visitor Services Section) at 827-2020 for further information on public education and recreational programs at the Mer Bleue Conservation Area. Further details on access limitation in the conservation area can be obtained at 239-5595.

Anonymous. (n.d.) The Greenbelt All Season Trail Map. National Capital Commission, Ottawa.

Anonymous. 1974. Proceedings of the Mer Bleue Seminar. Interpretation Section, National Capital Commission, Ottawa.

Ashley, S. 1979. Mer Bleue : The Evolution of an Urban Bog. Interpretation Service, National Capital Commission, Ottawa.

Baldwin, W.K.W. and T. Mosquin. 1969. Scientific and Cultural Studies of the Mer Bleue. Canadian Field-Naturalist 83: 4-6.

Brunton, D.F. 1984. The Vegetation and Flora of the Mer Bleue Conservation Area, National Capital Commission Greenbelt, Ottawa-Carleton, Ontario. Conservation Studies 22, National Capital Commission, Ottawa.

Cook, F.R. 1981. Amphibians and Reptiles of the Ottawa District. Trail & Landscape 15: 75-109.

# 29) Pine Grove Trail

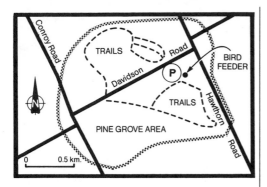

This young woodland is situated in moist to wet sand east of Blossom Park at Davidson and Hawthorn Roads in the National Capital Commission's Pine Grove Forest Reserve. It is part of the National Capital Greenbelt and although disturbed by logging, offers a pleasant walk through a variety of woodland habitats.

## Features:
Sand-loving spring wildflowers are abundant in the young mixed woods of Trembling Aspen, White Birch, Green Ash and Red Maple. Because of the variety of trees, including the White Pine for which the area is named, this is a good place for typical winter birds such as Black-capped Chickadee, Downy Woodpecker, White-breasted Nuthatch and Evening Grosbeak. The Ottawa Field Naturalists have managed a public bird feeder here for many winters to offer visitors the opportunity of seeing these birds at close range. In a shallow wetland about 100 m west of the feeder there is a small peatland. It supports a number of plants that are seldom seen in the Regional Municipality of Ottawa-Carleton, including the shrubs Sheep Laurel (Kalmia angustifolia) and Leatherleaf (Chamaedaphne calyculata) and her-

baceous plants such as Virginia Cotton-grass (Eriophorum virginicum). The surrounding landscape consists of large expanses of open farmland, thus increasing the value of this forest as an island of reasonably natural cover.

## Visiting:
The Pine Grove Trail is a self-guiding interpretive path through a Red Pine plantation and, as such, is of limited natural interest. Trail 2 south of Davidson Road will bring you to the bird feeder in winter and through a good cross-section of the woods in all seasons. There is year-round parking available and a picnic area and toilets too. You will need private transportation to the site. None of the trails are suitable for travel by wheelchair.

## Equipment and Considerations:
The frequency of wet spots along Trail 2 argues for sturdy, waterproof footwear. Insect repellent will likely be necessary in early summer. Binoculars are useful for observing bird life year-round, as is a camera for capturing spring wildflowers and the like.

## Seasonal Events & Suggestions:
**Spring** - wildflowers along the trail.
- common migrant woodland birds.

**Summer** - unusual plants of the peatland.
- common breeding birds of young hardwoods.

**Winter** - public bird feeder on Trail 2.
- tracks of common woodland mammals (including Red Squirrel, mice, Snowshoe Hare, etc.) in the woods.

## References:

Anonymous. (n.d.) The Greenbelt All Season Trail Map. National Capital Commission, Ottawa.

Brunton, D.F. 1984. Nature Reserve Potential and Management on National Capital Commission Lands in the National Capital Region, Ontario/Quebec. Conservation Studies 29, National Capital Commission, Ottawa.

Mosquin, T. and J. Gillett. 1985. Inventory and Evaluation of the Pine Grove and Carlsbad Springs Forest Reserves. Conservation Studies 34, National Capital Commission, Ottawa.

Pringle, G. 1986. Ottawa Region Bird Feeders for the Winter Season. Trail & Landscape 20: 206-208.

# 30) Cobb's Lake

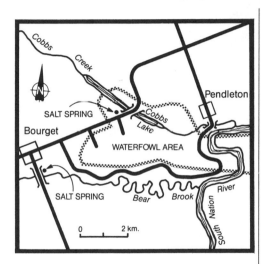

Five kilometers east of Bourget along the Bear Brook Road is a long, narrow, marshy pond that contains a number of curious and unlikely natural features that are very significant in the Capital area. They result from events as long ago as the Champlain Sea era and as recently as last spring's weather in the high arctic.

## Features:
The creek running through this lowland is the vestige of the once large river that emptied the post-glacial Great Lakes through the Ottawa Valley. The remaining valley is flat,

clay bottomed and slow to drain; it floods extensively each spring. This offers resting and staging grounds for vast numbers of Canada Geese and other waterfowl. These flocks number in the thousands - occasionally peaking at 100,000 or more - and often include a few rare species like Snow or Greater White-fronted Geese. This all happens in a short period at the peak of flood each spring. Later in the summer Cobb's Lake is stagnant and develops a rich aquatic vegetation. A small salt spring bubbles forth on the north side of the road. The concrete cistern in the field was used to capture mineral water from the spring for commercial purposes many years ago. (Such water was thought to be health-giving.) These salt waters result from 10,000 year old Champlain Sea salt being flushed out of deep sand deposits by otherwise normal groundwater. At least one plant found at the springs at Cobb's Lake requires this high salt content for its survival.The Seaside Buttercup (*Ranunculus cymbalaria*) may have been here for over 100 centuries and is very rare in southern Ontario. With it grows Walter's Barnyard Grass *(Echinochloa walteri)*, a southern species that is rare throughout its

175

Canadian range. A curious spot indeed !

**Visiting:**
The site can be reached along the Bear Brook Road at the Cobb's Lake overpass.Parking is available on the east side of the overpass by the lake (on the south side of the road). This is all private property and no public facilities are provided. The salt tolerant plants grow in the ditch along the north side of the road a little to the west of the overpass, so there is no need to enter the private lands. Waterfowl can be best observed from the highest point, which is along the overpass.

**Equipment and Considerations:**
The shoulder of Bear Brook Road is narrow so be very alert to on-coming traffic when standing at the roadside. Parking and access may be even more limited during peak flood periods in the spring. Binoculars are all but essential here and a spotting telescope is very useful too. The

otherwise uncommon Giant Ragweed *(Ambrosia trifida)* is abundant here. That is interesting botanically but bad news for hayfever sufferers in late summer. Full services can be found a few kilometers to the west at Bourget.

**Seasonal Events & Suggestions:**
**Spring** - vast waterfowl concentrations on flooded fields by the lake (varies with water level and period of spring runoff in late March and early April).
**Summer** - rare salt spring plants and uncommon weeds along the roadside by Cobb's Lake.
- rich aquatic vegetation in Cobb's Lake.

**References:**
Di Labio, B. M. 1987. Where to See Migrating Waterfowl East of Ottawa. Trail & Landscape 21: 88-92.

Dore, W.G. 1953. *Echinochloa walteri* re-instated in Ottawa District Flora. Canadian Field-Naturalist 67: 138.

# Other Areas

I said at the outset of this section that I was picking a selection of areas in the Capital that I felt expressed a cross-section of the natural life to be found here. There are many, many other areas that can also be profitably explored. The scope of this book precludes discussing them all. A number of such areas are described in other sources, however, and these are listed below. A literature reference (or references) follow(s) each listing. I'm sure some familiar names will appear. Perhaps this will encourage you to discover a little more about them.
The sites are listed in no particular

order within their municipal area, beginning with Quebec.

**Aylmer**
- Outaouais shore    (Gagnon 1980, Brunton 1984).

**Hull**
- Chelsea Clay Ravine (Gagnon 1980).
- Leamy Lake (Gagnon 1980).

**Ottawa**
- Sawmill Creek (Billington Tozer 1977, Brunton 1984).
- Frank Ryan Park (Dickson and Darbyshire 1979).
- Vincent Massey Park (Dickson and

Darbyshire 1979, Dickson 1982).

- Hampton Park (Billington and Tozer 1977).

- Champlain Bridge and Islands (Dickson and Darbyshire 1979, Brunton 1984).

- Rockcliffe Airbase Woods (Dickson and Darbyshire 1979, Brunton 1984).

- Lemieux Island (Dickson and Darbyshire 1979).

- Upper Duck Island (Dickson and Darbyshire 1979, Darbyshire 1981).

- Victoria Island (Dickson and Darbyshire 1979).

**Gloucester**
- McCarthy Woods (Dickson and Darbyshire 1979).

-Blossom Park Woods (Dickson and Darbyshire 1979).

- DND Woods (Brunton 1983).

- Blackburn Hamlet Woodlot (Brunton 1983).

- South Gloucester Woods (Dickson and Darbyshire 1979, Dugal 1978).

**West Carleton**
- Long Swamp Fen (Reddoch 1978, 1979, Taylor 1978).

- Morris Island (Dugal and Reddoch 1980).

The literature sources cited above are as follows:

Billington, C. and E.W. Tozer. 1977. Ecological Inventory of NCC Urban Corridors. Interpretation Section, National Capital Commission, Ottawa.

Brunton, D.F. 1983. An Ecological Inventory of the Green's Creek Sector of the National Capital Commission Greenbelt, Gloucester, Ontario. Conservation Studies 15, National Capital Commission, Ottawa.

Brunton, D.F. 1984. Nature Reserve Potential and Management in the National Capital Region on National Capital Commission Lands, Ontario/Quebec. Conservation Studies 29, National Capital Commission, Ottawa.

Darbyshire, S.J. 1981. Upper Duck and Lower Duck Islands. Trail & Landscape 15: 133-139.

Dickson, H.L. 1982. Vincent Massey Park and Area. Trail & Landscape 16: 106-110.

Dickson, H.L. and S.J. Darbyshire. 1979. Biological Inventories of 23 Areas in the Ottawa Region. Conservation Section, National Capital Commission, Ottawa.

Dugal, A. 1978. The South Gloucester Conservation Area Revisited. Trail & Landscape 12: 47-53.

Dugal, A. and J. Reddoch. 1980. Morris Island. Trail & Landscape 14: 18-23.

Gagnon, D. 1980. Inventaire des Ressouces Naturelles des Boises de la Region de Hull. Conservation Section, National Capital Commission, Ottawa.

Reddoch, J. 1978. The Long Swamp near Manion Corners. Trail & Landscape 12: 19- 23.

Reddoch, J. 1979. Calcareous Fens in the Ottawa District. Trail & Landscape 13: 16-27.

Taylor, R. 1978. Breeding Bird Excursion to Manion Corners Conservation Area. Trail & Landscape 12: 24-25.

# ADDITIONAL SOURCES AND ASSISTANCE

There is a tremendous wealth of information on the natural history of Canada's Capital available to anyone who wants it. We have been blessed with over a century of study by a large and expert body of naturalists - both professional and amateur - and their findings are open to us all. The only real difficulty for most people in using these materials is finding where they are and determining how to sort through them all. This section will help to answer some of those questions. It is important to remember, though, that these are only leads and that a far greater wealth of relevant resources are there to be discovered.

## 1) Organizations (General Interest)
A number of groups in the Capital area have an active interest in a broad spectrum of natural history subjects.

### THE OTTAWA FIELD-NATURALISTS' CLUB
This is the largest (over 2000 members and subscribers) and oldest (established 1879) naturalist group of its kind in Canada and is the premier organization for the field naturalist in the Ottawa Valley. It maintains an internationally recognized publication program through its official journal the *Canadian Field Naturalist*. Its local publication *Trail & Landscape* is less technical and aimed at the interested amateur in the Ottawa Valley. A regular series of outings is conducted year-round throughout the Capital area and beyond. Except for the summer months, monthly meetings are held for the benefit of members and the general public, covering a wide variety of natural history subjects. The OFNC is very active in local and provincial conservation programs. A 24 hour-a-day birding 'hot-line', offering recent sighting information and birding suggestions, is available (free) at 596-4888.
1987 membership cost-$17.00 (individual) or $19.00 (family). The address is Box 3264, Postal Station C, Ottawa K1Y 4J5 ; phone 722-3050 .

### MACNAMARA FIELD NATURALISTS' CLUB
This new club was established in 1984 by naturalists in the Arnprior area and maintains a very active program of outings and events in that city on the western fringe of the Capital. Monthly bulletins and a newsletter *(The Lady's-slipper)* are published. The club meets on the first Tuesday of each month at the Arnprior District High School. Organized field trips are conducted once a month (at least) on a wide range of natural history themes.
1987 membership cost-$8.00 (individual) or $12.00 (family) . The address is P.O. Box 94, Arnprior K7S 3H2 .

### CANADIAN PARKS AND WILDERNESS SOCIETY (Ottawa-Hull Chapter)
Long known as the National and Provincial Parks Association, this national body has been a strong advocate for environmental protection in parks across Canada. The Ottawa-Hull Chapter was formed around the issue of preserving wilderness values in Gatineau Park and it remains actively concerned with this and other parks in and about the Ottawa Valley. The chapter maintains an irregular schedule of

meetings and outings throughout the year, notice being given through their newsletter. All members receive *Borealis* (formerly *Park News*), the quarterly publication of the national organization.

1987 membership cost-$23.00 (individual), $28.00 (family) or $17.00 (student). The address for the Ottawa-Hull Chapter is Box 3072, Station D, Ottawa KlP 6H6.

## FEDERATION OF ONTARIO NATURALISTS

The FON is a provincial organization that has been active in promoting the conservation of Ontario's natural values since the 1930's . It publishes *Seasons*, a quarterly periodical that occasionally contains information on the Capital area and the Ottawa Valley. Its program of excursions and tours covers all of Ontario and occasionally includes the Capital area.

1987 membership cost-$26.00 (individual) or $32.00 (family). The address is 355 Lesmill Road, Don Mills M3B 2W8 ; phone (416)444-8419 .

## RIDEAU TRAIL ASSOCIATION

Established in 1971, this organization developed and maintains a 310 km walking trail between Ottawa and Kingston, paralleling the Rideau River. Concerned with non-mechanized, wild-country travel, the association conducts hikes along the Rideau Trail (or along some of the 78 kms of side trails) on a year-round basis. Though not specifically a natural history group, the organization has strongly allied interests and many cross memberships.

1987 membership cost $10.00 (individual or family). An Ottawa information line is maintained at 596-0572 . The mailing address is Box 15, Kingston K7L 4V6.

# 2) Organizations (Specialty Groups)

Several groups in and about Canada's Capital have interests in a particular facet of natural history study and appreciation.

## CLUB DES ORNITHOLOGES DE L'OUTAOUAIS

This francophone club was established in Hull in 1978 and is very active in western Quebec, conducting a wide-ranging series of outings across the Quebec portion of the Capital area. They maintain public winter bird feeders at a number of sites, including Leamy Lake Park, Beauchamp Lake Park, Pink Road (with the Ottawa Field Naturalists) and at Asticou in Gatineau Park. Their periodical, *L'ornitaouais*, is published three times a year ; the club also maintains a french language bird alert 'hot-line' (778-0737).

1987 membership cost $10.00 (individual), $14.00 (family) or $8.00 (student). The address is Box 419, Station A, Hull J8Y 6P2. Information on the club may also be obtained by calling 776-3822.

## ONTARIO FIELD ORNITHOLOGISTS

OFO was initiated in 1982 as a provincial organization to promote the conservation of birds, as well as the appreciation, scientific documentation and recreation of birding in Ontario. It conducts field trips across the province on a regular basis. Its publication, *Ontario Birds,* is published two or three times a year ; its content usually relates to conditions in the Ottawa Valley at least in part.

1987 membership cost-$13.00(individual). The address is Box 1204, Station B, Burlington L7P 3S9.

**FIELD BOTANISTS OF ONTARIO**
Established in 1984, this provincial organization encourages the study of botany throughout the province and has conducted a number of general excursion meetings. Regional field trips, including ones in and about the Capital, are undertaken annually. A newsletter is periodically distributed to the members.

1987 membership cost-$8.00 (individual). The address is c/o Mr. D. Geddes, 44 Massey Street, Bramalea L6S 2V8.

# 3) Public Institutions and Services
We are especially blessed in Canada's Capital with public research institutions that can greatly assist in private investigations of the natural world. A number of the most important for the naturalist are described below.

## NATIONAL MUSEUM OF NATURAL SCIENCES
The well-known Victoria Memorial Museum on Metcalfe Street is only the public tip of the iceberg for this remarkable institution. For many years its scientists and naturalists have been studying the natural history of Canada, developing literally irreplaceable collections of specimens and artifacts as well as superb libraries. Most importantly, the specialists at the Museum are walking encyclopedias of knowledge in their fields and are always ready to help newcomers and serious students alike.

**i) Interpretive Facilities** - the Victoria Museum contains exhibits on natural history themes for the whole of Canada, but often uses Capital area scenes and situations as examples. Visitors can obtain a good introduction to the larger groups of flora and fauna of the Capital and Canada by a visit (or visits) to this marvellous facility.

**ii) Research Collections** - the collections of natural history specimens outgrew the facilities at the Victoria Museum years ago and they and the Museum's scientific staff are housed in a variety of buildings in the Capital. Separate collections of specimens are maintained for many specialties, including :
- vascular and non-vascular plants
- birds
- mammals
- fish
- reptiles and amphibians
- fossils

While these research facilities are not generally open to the public because of the need for protection and security for the specimens, individuals with particular interests or questions can often arrange a visit by contacting the curator of the particular collection(s). These collections are extremely useful learning tools; no book can replace the real thing and the first-hand knowledge of the scientists who study them. In addition to the collections themselves, libraries are maintained that can be consulted on the same basis as the collections. Phone 996-3102 for information on contacting the appropriate persons in the individual collection(s).

## BIOSYSTEMATICS RESEARCH CENTRE (BRC)

Despite its ponderous name this important research facility of Agriculture Canada offers much to the non-expert and even casually curious individual. The BRC maintains an identification service as part of its mandate and will identify agriculturally related plant and insect specimens, where possible. Their facilities in the Neatby Building (insects) and the Saunders Building (plants) at the Central Experimental Farm can greatly assist one in developing a good personal knowledge of natural science features in Canada's Capital.

Two major portions of the Centre are of greatest interest for most naturalists:

i) Entomology - although primarily concerned with agricultural research, some of the important pure research activities have resulted in collections of interest for the less scientifically inclined. The Canadian National Insect Collection, containing over 13,000,000 specimens, is housed here and includes a complete collection of Canadian butterflies, moths, dragonflies and beetles, as well as less widely enjoyed insects such as black flies, mosquitoes and deer flies ! The largest group of entomologists in Canada works at the BRC.

ii) Botany - as with the entomologists, the botanists and mycologists at the BRC are primarily involved in agriculturally related studies, although pure research is also carried on. The vascular plant herbarium contains over 800, 000 specimens, by far the greatest number of any Canadian collection. The national mycology collection holds some 250,000 specimens of fungi in the same building. The scientists are open to requests for help and consultation. All of the specialists at the BRC can be reached at 996-1665.

## OTTAWA PUBLIC LIBRARY

The public library system, dating from the early days of Ottawa, has built a wealth of information on all aspects of Canada's Capital since the pre-confederation era.

Most standard biological references are available at the library (if not at branch libraries then at the central building on Metcalfe Street) and inter-library loans can accommodate volumes not on the shelves there. It also maintains a variety of other useful information services and can be a valuable starting point in developing references and information.

The number of the central switchboard is 236-0301.

## CARLETON AND OTTAWA UNIVERSITIES

Both of the major universities in Ottawa have biology departments in which academic instruction, scientific research and public education activities are conducted.

i) **Public Education** - both universities run courses in their continuing education programs that are botanically related, although these tend to concentrate on wildflower identification rather than field identification of the total flora and fauna. The greenhouses at Carleton University, called ELBA, display a variety of exotic and native habitats that can be visited by the public (free) on a year-round basis.

ii) **Research Consultation** - faculty members who are authorities in a variety of botanical and zoological fields are on staff at the two universities; both institutions also maintain small biological collections for teaching purposes.

## BOARDS OF EDUCATION

Each year continuing education courses are taught on a wide variety of natural history topics including birdwatching, wildflower identification, etc. The courses are set up in response to public demand so they can be structured to meet needs and interests. There are modest charges for these courses, usually intended to cover basic costs only. The numbers for the continuing education offices are as follows:

Ottawa Board - 653-2325.
Carleton Board - 596-8225.

## ONTARIO MINISTRY OF NATURAL RESOURCES (OMNR)

As the provincial department responsible for natural resources management in Ontario, OMNR maintains a great deal of information on wildlife species, provincial park resources, forestry and so on. Staff at the Carleton Place District office concerned with these subjects can often help with questions or can direct you to the appropriate resources. The Eastern Regional office in Kemptville has a Regional Ecologist who can answer many questions regarding provincial parks, areas of natural and scientific interest (ANSI's) and crown lands.

The District office number in Carleton Place is 836-1237; the Regional Ecologist can be reached in Kemptville at 258-8354 (long distance from Ottawa).

## CONSERVATION AUTHORITIES

The Rideau Valley and Mississippi Valley Conservation Authorities maintain interpretive facilities (and staff) that can be of considerable help to visitors. Some of these are identified in the Places to See section (such as Baxter Conservation Area and the Mill of Kintail) but other programs and facilities are available on a wide variety of topics - usually at no cost. It is best to contact the Authority in question and request information on their program for the coming season.

The Rideau Valley Conservation Authority number (in Manotick) is 692-3571.

The Mississippi Valley Conservation Authority number (in Lanark) is 1-800-267-1659.

## NATIONAL CAPITAL COMMISSION (NCC)

The NCC conducts management and interpretive studies on federal lands in the National Capital Region and can provide information on many of these areas. A wide range of visitor services including interpretation programs and information centers is also offered by the Commission.

i) **Visitor Services** - interpretive facilities and exhibits as well as public programming are provided at several sites in the Capital by the NCC. An interpretation centre at Stony Swamp Conservation Area and the Gatineau Park visitor center are examples; both carry a wide range of free pamphlets as well as trail maps for sale. NCC staff can be hired to conduct groups into such areas as the Mer Bleue and Stony Swamp Conservation Areas or Gatineau Park. It is best to contact the National Capital Visitor Center (239-5000) to see what programs will be available, and where, in the coming season.

ii) **Resource Information** - the Conservation Section maintains information on the natural resources of conservation areas and other federal lands in the Capital. These reports and files can often be obtained free of charge, or particular questions on federal lands can be answered by a staff member. The phone number for the Conservation Section is 239-5595.

A wide variety of continuing education courses are offered, usually at minimal cost to the participants, by the community colleges in Ottawa and Hull. These include birdwatching, wildflower identification, and a number of other courses that are geared to the novice or more advanced levels of understanding. Contact the continuing education office of your appropriate community college for further details.

# 4) Literature Resources

There are books written as guides to the natural history literature of the Capital, there is that much of it! It would obviously be impractical to try to list even a small portion of those titles. The most important items, those that can serve as a first line of attack for further study, are listed below. The following general groupings are employed:
- **General Natural History (periodicals)**
- **General Natural History (books)**
- **Botany**
- **Birds**
- **Mammals**
- **Amphibians and Reptiles**
- **Fish**
- **Butterflies**

## General Natural History (periodicals)

*Trail & Landscape* (1967 - ) - four issues each year are devoted to exploration of natural history in the Ottawa Valley; the primary modern source of natural history information on the Capital; available to all members of The Ottawa Field-Naturalists' Club (back issues are also sold through that organization); a 20-year index (1967-1986) was published in 1987.

*The Canadian Field Naturalist* (1880 - ) - the premier natural sciences journal in Canada, with over a century of publication to its credit ; contains invaluable historical material on early natural history discoveries and studies in the Capital ; now a more national journal in scope and local items are less frequent; an index to the earliest volumes (1880 - 1919) was published by The Ottawa Field-Naturalists' Club in 1980 ; the journal is available to all members of that club, as well as to subscribers around the world on a quarterly basis. Back issues are available at a nominal cost from The Ottawa Field-Naturalists' Club (see page 179).

*Seasons* (1960 - ) long known as the Ontario Naturalist, it is received by all members of the Federation of Ontario Naturalists; contains popularized treatments of various topics concerning natural history and conservation in Ontario; occasionally includes articles directly discussing Ottawa Valley areas and features.

## General Natural History (books)

**Several books offer important keys to the biological literature and natural history of relevance to the Capital, including the following:**

Muhammad, A.F. & E. Jorgensen. 1974. Natural History in the National Capital Region. Information Report FMR-X-65, Department of the Environment, Ottawa.

Gillett, J.M. 1980. Transactions of the Ottawa Field-Naturalists' Club and the Ottawa Naturalist Index. Special Publication 2, Ottawa Field-Naturalists' Club, Ottawa.

Gummer, W.K. 1987. Trail & Landscape Cumulative Index Volumes 1-20.(1967-1986). Ottawa Field-Naturalists' Club, Ottawa.

National Capital Commission. (1980 -    ) Conservation Studies Series(1 - ). Greenbelt Division, NCC, Ottawa.

Peterkin, P. 1981 (Editor). Rideau Trail Notes. Rideau Trail Association, Ottawa.

## Botany
**Several important botanical references for the Capital area are:**

Fernald, M.L. 1950. Gray's Manual of Botany (Eighth Edition). American Book Company, Boston.

Gleason, H.A. 1968. The New Britton and Brown Illustrated Flora of the northeastern United States and adjacent Canada (3 volumes). New York Botanical Garden, New York.

Marie-Victorin, Frere. 1964. Flore laurentienne (Second Edition). Presses de l'Universite de Montreal, Montreal.

  Voss, E.G. 1972 and 1985. Michigan Flora - Volumes 1 and 2. Cranbrook Institute of Science, Bloomfield Hills.

**These are technical manuals intended for professionals and serious non-professionals.  Gleason, Fernald and Marie-Victorin are well respected standards but are rather dated. Voss's books are terrific, but cover only a part of our flora. Two useful non-technical references for plant identification are:**

McKay, S. & P. Catling. 1979. Trees, Shrubs and Flowers to Know in Ontario. J.M. Dent & Sons, Toronto.

Peterson, R.T. - The Peterson Field Guides - series of field guides (with other authors) on wildflowers, ferns, trees and shrubs.

**Other useful general publications include:**

Hosie, R.C. 1969. Native Trees of Canada. Environment Canada, Ottawa.

Soper, J.H. & M.L. Heimburger. 1982. Shrubs of Ontario. Royal Ontario Museum, Toronto.

Dore, W.G. & J. McNeill. 1980. The Grasses of Ontario. Agriculture Canada, Ottawa.

Whiting, R.E. & P.M. Catling. 1986. Orchids of Ontario. CanaColl Foundation, Ottawa.

Semple, J.C.and G.S. Ringius. 1983. The Goldenrods of Ontario. Dept. of Biology, University of Waterloo, Waterloo.

Semple, J.C. and S.B. Heard 1987. The Asters of Ontario. Dept. of Biology, University of Waterloo, Waterloo.

Frankton, C. & G. Mulligan. 1970. Weeds of Canada. Agriculture Canada, Ottawa.

**Botanical literature that directly describes the flora of the Capital include:**

Gillett, J.M. and D.J. White. 1978. Checklist of Vascular Plants of the Ottawa-Hull Region, Canada. National Museum of Natural Sciences, Ottawa.

Dore, W.G. 1959. Grasses of the Ottawa District. Publication 1049, Canada Department of Agriculture, Ottawa.

Dobson, I. & P. Catling. 1983. Pondweeds *(Potamogeton)* of the Ottawa District. Trail & Landscape 17:79-99.

Cody, W.J. 1978. Ferns of the Ottawa District (Revised). Publication 974, Canada Department of Agriculture, Ottawa.

# Birds
There is a very rich literature on birds in Canada. A few of the major references are listed below :

Godfrey, W.E.G. 1986. The Birds of Canada (Second Edition). National Museum of Natural Sciences, Ottawa.

Peterson, R.T. 1980. A Field Guide to the Birds (Fourth Edition). Houghton Mifflin, Boston.

Scott, S.L. (Editor). 1983. Field Guide to the Birds of North America. National Geographic Society, Washington.

**References that relate particularly to the Capital area include the following :**

Cadman, M.D.,P. Eagles and F. Helleiner. 1987. Atlas of the Breeding Birds of Ontario. University of Waterloo Press, Waterloo.

OFNC. 1985. A Birder's Checklist of Ottawa. Ottawa Field-Naturalists' Club, Ottawa.

Pringle, G. 1986. Ottawa Region Bird feeders for the Winter Season. Trail & Landscape 20: 206-208.

Lloyd, H. 1944. The Birds of Ottawa, 1944. Canadian Field-Naturalist 58:143-175.

# Mammals
**The most important references to mammals in this general area include :**

Banfield, A.W.F. 1974. The Mammals of Canada. University of Toronto Press, Toronto.

Burt, W.H. 1964. A Field Guide to the Mammals. Houghton Mifflin, Boston.

Murie, O.J. 1965. A Field Guide to Animal Tracks. Houghton Mifflin, Boston.

Peterson, R.L. 1966. The Mammals of Eastern Canada. Oxford University Press, Toronto.

**The only comprehensive mammal report for the Capital area is an old one :**

Rand, A.L. 1945. The Mammals of the Ottawa District. Canadian Field-Naturalist 59:111-132.

# Amphibians and Reptiles
**Some of the general literature useful in this area includes :**

Cook, F.R. 1984. Introduction to Canadian Amphibians and Reptiles. National Museum of Natural Sciences, Ottawa.

Conant, R. 1975. A Field Guide to Reptiles and Amphibians of Eastern and Central North America (Second Edition). Houghton Mifflin, Boston.

Smith, H.M. & E.D. Brodie. 1982. A Guide to Field Identification: Reptiles of North America. Golden Press, New York.

Smith, H.M. 1978. A Guide to Field Identification : Amphibians of North America. Golden Press, New York.

**The best review of amphibians and reptiles in the Capital is :**

Cook, F.R. 1981. Amphibians and Reptiles of the Ottawa Area (Revised Edition). Trail & Landscape 15:75-109.

# Fish
**While the literature on sport fish species is a very large one, a few key references can be identified as important sources of information on all species :**

Scott, W.B. and E.J. Crossman. 1973. Freshwater Fishes of Canada. Bulletin 184, Fisheries Research Board, Environment Canada, Ottawa.

MacKay, H.H. 1963. Fishes of Ontario. Ontario Department of Lands & Forests. Toronto.

**Excellent reviews of the fishes of the area can be found in the following references:**

Coad, B.W. 1987. Checklist of the Fishes of the Ottawa District. Trail & Landscape 21:40-60.

McAllister, D.E. and B.W. Coad. 1974. Fishes of Canada's National Capital. Fisheries Research Board of Canada, Ottawa.

## Butterflies

**A huge literature on butterflies exists but several key general references can be identified :**

Howe, W.H. 1975. Butterflies of North America. Doubleday & Sons, Garden City.

Klots, A.B. 1951. A Field Guide to the Butterflies of North America East of the Great Plains. Houghton Mifflin, Boston.

**The best source of local information is found in :**

Layberry, R.A., J.D. Lafontaine and P. Hall. 1982. Butterflies of the Ottawa District. Trail & Landscape 16:3-59.

# DO'S AND DON'TS

Most of us go into the natural world as strangers, visitors to a landscape and an environment with which we are really not familiar. Thus we should consider how to go about it before charging into a situation that may become a problem for ourselves or others. In this section I am offering some general ideas and hints to help individuals get the most out of a visit to the natural environment without causing undue wear and tear on themselves or the landscape. The most important advice I can offer, however, is as obvious as it is appropriate ... *use common sense* . A level head and a sense of respect combine wonderfully in unfamiliar situations.

## 1) APPROACH

### An Attitude of Respect

Although Canada's Capital is unusually well endowed with marvellous, still natural and wild areas, most of the landscape has felt the hand - and foot - of man. Those patches of naturalness are increasingly important, increasingly hard to replace, and increasingly threatened. It would be the most perverse of ironies if important natural areas were damaged by well-meaning visitors who came only to celebrate the features and values of the place. An old cliche about natural areas that you will hear in many reserves in North America is "Take only pictures, leave only footprints".

It is not enough to just enjoy what is to be seen and experienced in the wonderful natural areas of Canada's Capital, each visitor has a responsibility to use the area and its resources as they might the home of a friend. Just as you would not leave garbage around a friend's living room, you should not consider leaving litter in natural areas. It is self-evident, of course, but only if you think in terms of personal responsibility. So when visiting a spot to view a  stand of wildflowers, for example, take care not to damage surrounding plants while looking at or photographing the blooms. You can extend that to fit the million and one interesting situations you will encounter in such areas.

And *please*, do not try to find a "use" for everything. While the sampling of wild plants and animals for food or herbal remedies is tolerable in small quantities, it can be very destructive. These plants and animals have a more important role in the natural environment than they have as curiosity food items for humans.

It may sound trite but to paraphrase canoeist extraordinaire Omer Stringer, "if it hurts, you're doing it wrong". In other words, be prepared to have fun. While experiencing some places and features of the natural world can demand a lot of effort from visitors, it should all be within limits. Try to anticipate possible obstacles and bring along the materials or supplies that mitigate them. The important and delicate natural landscape is no place for someone to prove how tough they are; the bull-of-the-woods approach benefits neither the landscape nor the visitor.

### Seasonal Considerations

Each area changes from season to season and to fully appreciate what it has to offer you should anticipate some of the requirements of, or options available to, visitors. Your **clothing**, for example, should be as quiet as possible. Some synthetic materials make a terrible din in the quiet of winter forests. It should be layered; that is, wear a series of lighter coverings that can be peeled off or added on in cooler

189

seasons rather than a single, heavier piece. I find that a sweater, down vest and windbreaker shell cover just about all conditions, save the really cold periods of mid-winter when I retreat into a parka. You should also consider safety in autumn outings: be sure to wear bright colours in areas where hunting may be going on that make it apparent that you are not a game species!

Sturdy **footwear** is so important. A pair of Kodiak-type boots is a good all-around bush boot, though you might well wish for a warmer mukluk or snowmobile type boot in winter. The mukluks are more versatile in that they can easily be worn on snowshoes. Rubber boots in spring are good for short periods but can irritate your feet if you try to walk too long in them. For really wet places like bogs and marshes I find it best to accept the inevitable right away; I wear an old pair of sneakers - my "bog boots" - and don't even try to keep dry. Having dry footwear available at the end of such a hike is recommended, however.

A good **hat** is a real joy. While style is a personal thing, some kind of brim is highly recommended - especially if you wear glasses. A baseball style cap is quite effective for keeping rain, spider webs and miscellaneous other items off lenses. The important thing is that your hat effectively cuts the sun glare and protects your scalp from twigs and the best efforts of deer-flies to chew you to pieces.

# 2) EQUIPMENT

There are chains of stores that exist on servicing the interests of hikers and naturalists; the subject is far too large to cover completely here. I will just hit some of the high points, as it were, and offer some recommendations for gear which has served me well in my wanderings.

## Optical Equipment

A good pair of **binoculars** is essential for anyone wanting to observe wildlife on anything more than the most casual basis. By 'good' I do not mean high powered and high priced models that do all but identify the animal for you. Simple 7 x 35 or 7 x 50 power (7 times magnification with a 35 mm or 50 mm objective lens) do very well indeed. Higher powered binoculars usually are heavier, require brighter lighting conditions, are harder to hold still and/or do not focus in very closely. Although not good for the equipment, by the way, keeping your binoculars out of the case (either around your neck or in your hand) will ensure that you see more birds and other rapidly moving animals. Most birders, in fact, dispose of the binocular case when they bring the glasses home from the store.

A **spotting telescope** is a great help for viewing distant wildlife, especially waterfowl well out in wetlands and rivers. It is best kept on a collapsible tripod, ready for immediate use when you are in the appropriate habitat. Magnifications of between 20 and 40 power are widely used. Much less than that and you are not gaining much over binoculars; much more and you have problems with atmospheric disturbances (e.g. heat waves), steadiness, and lack of brightness.

A less exotic,inexpensive optical tool that I find to be of great value is a **10x hand lens**. It is helpful in identifying many plant and animal species (especially grasses and sedges) and also offers spectacular insights into the beauties of the small forms of life all around us. It can fit into a pocket or can easily be carried on a ribbon slung around your neck.

Photography is a wonderful way to retain your memories of interesting places and experiences as well as documenting rare or unusual species and situations. When considering a **camera** for use in the natural landscape you should keep in mind that the instamatic type is usually not satisfactory. More detail is required in most cases and for that a 35 mm single lens reflex camera is necessary. A normal (ca. 50 mm) lens can produce surprisingly satisfactory results without running up huge costs. While one can get very technical (and expensive) with all this, one or two special lenses can help a great deal. A wide-angle (ca. 28 - 35 mm) lens for example, does wonders for landscape and habitat photography. Add a couple of extension tubes to your normal lens and you have a moderate telephoto, without undue loss of brightness and clarity. A polarizing filter to soften glare can enhance landscape photography considerably. Beyond that, well, there are whole libraries on techniques and equipment.

## General Gear

The basic clothing requirement is addressed in Seasonal Considerations (page 189) but as a general rule of thumb I suggest wearing durable, light-weight clothing that you are willing to get dirty and wet. In that way you can concentrate on the landscape, not your apparel. Almost as part of the clothing, however, a small **day pack** should be taken along. It can hold a wonderful array of stuff like binoculars, a camera, first aid kit, a compass, field guide(s) ... and lunch. It also serves as a fine pillow when some wonderfully quiet spot requires greater consideration(!). Be sure the pack has small outside pockets so that you need not open the main pack every time you want to use some small item. A waist strap, which helps reduce the bouncing of the pack as you walk along, will be appreciated for long hikes.

One of the most useful items I take along in my pack is a supply of small plastic garbage bags. They serve a million and one purposes, such as keeping my lunch dry and in one piece, carrying small, related bits of equipment and carrying out garbage. They are also excellent for carrying plant specimens and other artifacts out of the field. (Be sure to observe any limitations on collecting, however - see Hazards and Concerns section, page 192). A sturdy hunting knife is a helpful all-around tool. A compass and a couple of granola bars are always good to have along, just in case you become misplaced(!).

## Records and Information

In the Additional Sources and Assistance section (page 184), books and other literature are cited that can help you in developing a particular interest. In the field, however, there is no substitute for an observer who takes careful notes. These can be compared with literature and other sources of information at a later date and often yield applications that were not even considered when the events were recorded. A **notebook** stuffed in a back pocket and a pencil in hand will repay the minimal costs incurred many times over. A pencil or indelible ink pen are better than regular pens which can run, smear or wash away. A word of caution (at the insistence of my wife); indelible pens can make an awful mess of your clothes if the pen top comes off!

The careful collection of **biological specimens** is an excellent way to gather information that will last for generations -even centuries. Most field guides include sections on how to secure specimens. This is not a simple thing to do in many circumstances, however. There are legal constraints on collecting in many areas (see Hazards and Concerns section, page 192). Just as importantly, serious damage can result from inexpert if well-meaning collections. As a general rule of thumb, DO NOT collect specimens if a photograph will do AND until you are sufficiently familiar with the techniques required to make superior collections. Don't forget the value of well-kept notes.

## Maps

For most purposes, excellent **field maps** can be found in the 1:50,000 scale National Topographic Map series (NTS maps) They are published by Energy,Mines and Resources Canada (available at the Information and Sales Center, Logan Building, 580 Booth Street, Ottawa ; phone 995-4510; $4.00/map in 1987). Each map shows roads, trails and even forested areas as well as basic topographic and cultural features. Most of the areas I have mentioned are to be found on sheets 31 G/5 (Ottawa), 31 G/6 (Russell), 31 F/8 (Arnprior) and 31 G/12 (Wakefield).

# 3) HAZARDS AND CONCERNS

## Legalities

As a minimum, you should be sure that the area in which you wish to explore is legally available to the public. Provincial laws regarding access to private property, for example, must be respected. Similarly, crossing private property to get to a water body for fishing may not be permissible without the approval of the owner. It is the responsibility of the individual to know the rules in this regard. As a good rule of thumb, when you are in doubt, DO NOT ENTER. A good review of the Ontario Trespass Act as it relates to naturalists is to be found in the 1980 article in *Trail & Landscape* 14:128-129 .

Municipal and Regional jurisdictions also put limitations on what can and cannot be done on some publicly owned land. It is a good idea to contact the appropriate office to see what, if any, restrictions apply to the area(s) you wish to explore. Similarly, wildlife management regulations like fishing licenses, collection permits, access fees, etc. should be considered to avoid inconvenience and potential embarrassment.

Collecting of biological specimens is prohibited in provincial parks, park reserves and on National Capital Commission lands without a permit. In addition, any plant or animal listed under the Endangered Species Act of Ontario is protected from disturbance.

## Bugs, Blisters, Bruises and Breakdowns

Not to belabour the point but there are a number of things you should consider to ensure a happy and healthy experience in the wilder lands of Canada's Capital.

Biting insects are certainly a well-known nuisance for outdoor activities in summer. In the Capital area, however, they are rarely a serious problem for more than a short period. Perhaps the most dreaded is the **black fly,** actually several species of tiny, blackish flies which emerge from larvae in fresh, fast-running water mostly in the spring and early summer. They are active only in the day-time (mercifully) and can usually be held off by a combination of insect repellent and light-coloured clothing. Black flies are attracted to certain colours - especially blue and maroon. The worst is over by mid-June. Black flies are often abundant around blueberries (which they pollinate) and are most common in the Gatineau Hills with its multitude of small, fast streams.

The **mosquito,** another pesky summer insect, becomes common just about the time that the black flies have passed their worst! There are actually 40 species of mosquitoes in the Capital area (glad to hear that, aren't you ?), the majority of which attack large mammals, including us. The blood extracted is not for food but serves as a nutrient for the female's developing eggs. The male does not bite. Insect repellent and layered clothing usually keep mosquitoes at bay. Unfortunately, mosquitoes are active day and night and are especially common near areas of shallow, still water where their larvae can develop. By late summer, however, they become a minor problem for most people. For a more complete discussion of local mosquitoes and their natural history, refer to the article in *Trail & Landscape 15:152-155 (1981)*.

**Bees, wasps and hornets** are painfully definite in their dislike of being disturbed by humans. A sting or two is rarely a problem but if you are overly sensitive to their toxins or have never been stung before, beware. In the very rare cases of extreme sensitivity, individuals can become extremely ill and require immediate medical attention. Emergency adrenalin kits should be carried in the field by those who know that they are allergic.

A personal nemesis of mine is **deer flies** and their associated pest, **horse flies**. The deer fly is a housefly-sized, orange and black insect that flies at great speed and is capable of taking out painfully large chunks of flesh at a single "sitting". It, like its larger, gray associate the horse fly, largely ignores insect repellent and can penetrate alarmingly thick layers of clothing. Deer flies and horse flies are common in open, dry areas in mid-summer. An effective deterrent in my experience is a sturdy cap - a useful thing to have in hot, mid-summer places anyway. Both of these flies seem to key into the uppermost part of the body. Not being particularly bright, they will chew away at the top of a cap for the longest time, ignoring the exposed flesh of face and neck only a few centimeters below.

We have our share of **spiders** and insects that offer uncomfortable stings and bites, but such events are not common and are rarely serious. We are not bothered by the chiggers, ticks and other such nasties that infest areas to the west and south. As a good general rule, if you or a field companion become ill or physically uncomfortable in an unfamiliar way following insect bites, contact your family physician immediately. Don't risk the slight chance of a serious allergic reaction.

There are no poisonous **snakes** in Canada's Capital or anywhere in the Ottawa Valley, for that matter. There are a number of **poisonous plants**, but most of them offer no serious threat because of the amount required before toxic reactions occur, the awful taste, or the relative rarity of the species. Although you should be careful about eating or tasting wild berries that are unfamiliar to you - i.e. DON'T - there is a far greater risk from exotic weeds and house and garden plants. This is especially true for small children. Mushrooms should never be eaten unless their identity and quality is certain. As a rule of thumb, I confine my munchings to such certainties as blueberries, raspberries, strawberries and the like. I leave the rest to the creatures that *really* know what is good to eat in the natural world. Remember, what one person can eat without difficulty can make another seriously ill.

Any problem with wild plant poisoning - even if only suspected - should be immediately directed to the POISON CENTER at 521-4040.

You should be alert to other toxic reactions from plants. **Poison-ivy** is a common and troublesome plant that is especially abundant in limestone areas. It sprawls across dry, rocky or sandy sites where it can get lots of sunlight. Many people (unhappily, myself included) have extreme sensitivity to the oils found in *all* parts of the plant. The resulting allergic reaction can cause extensive, unbelievably itchy rashes to develop. Unless you know that you are not allergic to Poison-ivy, be sure to wash all body and clothing areas that were exposed to the plant as soon as possible. The toxic oil can retain its potency for months so be careful to clean off shovels and other tools that have contacted the plant before putting them away for fall storage. If you are unfortunate enough to contract the rash, contact your family physician for assistance. And learn how to identify it in the field (see page 41); five minutes of study can save hours or days of discomfort.

It is always a good idea to carry a basic **first aid kit** when venturing far off roadways. A few bandages, some disinfectant, a roll of tape and some sturdy string all sealed up in a plastic bag should do. In winter be sure to have a sleeping bag or blankets and some food in your car, just in case you get stuck or have engine failure in some out-of-the-way spot. Having some **cold-weather survival gear** in your car (including candles and matches) is a good idea in winter. An **axe**, by the way, is a wonderful all-around tool for surmounting all sorts of difficulties. I keep one in my vehicle on a year-round basis, right there with the shovel and tire jack.

It is very important to let someone know where you are going if you plan to be away for an extended period in a seldom-travelled area; this can save a whole lot of grief in an emergency.

It is important to realize that the natural world moves to the beat of its own drummer. When we are travelling through a natural landscape, *we* are the strangers. Nature is not something to be beaten back, wrestled down or over come. Neither is it a threatening force. As strangers in the natural world, however, we should act with the degree of respect, attention and preparation that we would in an unknown human community. If you consider yourself a guest here, and act accordingly, you and the natural landscape will both emerge the better for the experience.

# DEVELOPMENT OF THE LANDSCAPE

From the descriptions in this book and from visits to various natural areas, it becomes obvious that Canada's Capital has a complex and diverse landscape. But it has not always been as we see it now. The present landscape is the result of thousands of millions of years of evolution, of massive environmental change, of untold multitudes of living things each adding their bit. While much of that great history is obscure, a surprising amount is known of the conditions that were here in the distant past. In the following pages I offer a brief description of the origins and evolution of the natural landscape in the Capital. At the end is a selected bibliography of the literature from which the story is extracted. As the description progresses, I have included the reference number for the area or areas in the Places to See section that illustrate the point being discussed. The notation (2d), for example, directs readers to the Mackenzie King Estate description and (19) refers to the Britannia Conservation Area. From these references you can visit real examples of the evidence for this landscape evolution story.

## Evolution of the Land

Our landscape began forming with sedimentation of minute bits of minerals and sand into ancient seas. These materials were eventually transformed into sandstone and limestone rock. Then, under the extraordinary pressure and heat of mountain building activity, they were transformed again into the extremely hard, erosion resistant granite and gneiss (pronounced 'nice') that characterize most of the Gatineau Hills and much of the vast Canadian Shield (1,2,8,14) . Bands of marble, the result of metamorphosis of the limestone, cross the Shield landscape (2c, 2e). Throughout this time there was also much volcanic activity in the area. For hundreds of millions of years, starting well over one *billion* years ago, these rocks were forming, transforming, being covered and re-exposed, all combining to form the great mass of ancient Precambrian Canadian Shield that rises so dramatically along the northern side of the lowlands in Canada's Capital (2b). Were one to witness the scene it would appear totally alien: smoking volcanoes obscuring the sun; no plant or animal life (all life was confined to the oceans); a bleak, almost lunar landscape of crumbling rock, gravel slopes and lava.

It took untold millions of years before significant changes in this uninviting picture took place. The erosional influence of wind and water and changing temperatures ever so slowly broke the rock into smaller particles. Although the landscape here remained a dry, mountainous one, the products of erosion built up over the millennia. When subsequent changes in the earth's crust resulted in the area being submerged by ocean waters, major changes followed.

A deep depression (the Ottawa - St. Lawrence Basin) was formed by the continuing distortion of the earth's crust in the lower Ottawa and upper St. Lawrence Valleys. As the sea flooded in from the great troughs that occupied what was to be the Appalachian Mountains, the erosional material from the aging, declining mountains to the north covered its floor. These deposits, a mere 450 - 500 million years old(!), built up and later became stone. From this resulted the deposits of limestone, dolomite and sandstone that characterize much of the Capital area off the Canadian

Shield (6, 12, 16, 21, 23, 25). This pattern continued, with periods when the seas receded eastward and exposed the land for a time, until hundreds of meters of sandstone, limestone, sand, gravel and other deposits had built up.

The land rose from the sea once more about 300 - 400 million years ago. Extensive deposition continued in this part of the world, fueled by continuing erosion by wind and water. The shallow, warm seas in what is now western Canada were developing coal and oil deposits while scouring winds and blazing sun slowly broke down the exposed bedrock that covered much of our landscape.

In this period too, sea life was developing more sophisticated forms and plant life was spreading into the swamps and up onto the land. The first amphibious animals, ancient relatives of our frogs and reptiles, moved up from the sea. By about 200 million years ago dinosaurs were the dominant animal group. Another 140 million years were to pass before mammals became dominant and dinosaurs died out. Plant life evolved too, no longer just resembling primitive ferns and their allies, but developing into many of the groups and forms that we know today. During this period movements in the earth's crust slowly pushed up the land to the east, forming what we now know as the Appalachian Mountains and causing great cracks and faults to form in the bedrock of our area. Some of these resulted in massive cliffs and escarpments while others formed distinctive ridges across the landscape (2b, 2c, 14, 21 , 25), changing the drainage patterns in parts of the area. This altered the topography and increased the diversity of habitats available to a growing number of plants and animals.

By the modern era our landscape had undergone a long history of cataclysmic events, unceasing erosion and periods of prolonged flooding and marine deposition. It had a complex geological make-up as well as a diverse set of ground conditions. The mighty mountain ranges of the Shield were much reduced and the Basin below was deeply buried in softer, richer materials. The stage was set for a dramatic series of events that put the final touches on the evolution of our landscape.

# Glaciation

We don't know how many glacial periods affected the Capital area but it is clear that there were several during the last one million years. While the evidence of earlier glacial periods is obscure much can be determined about the last one. In any case, the plant and animal life of the Capital and most of Canada effectively dates only from the end of that last glaciation, since the entire area had been covered by a thick layer of ice for thousands of years.

A continental glaciation is a long term climatic event, resulting from slightly cooler-than-normal global climates. Why this happens in the first place is not completely clear, but it likely results in part from periodically altered rotational patterns of the earth around the sun. Simply put however, a glacier develops when the summer melt is insufficient to remove the ice and snow laid down by the previous winter. Given a continuing pattern of this and lots of time, the snow builds up, compressing lower layers into ice. The ice eventually begins to flow out from the point of build up. It takes many centuries for such a glacier to engulf an area the size of Canada, but that is precisely what has happened several times during the last one million years.

The last great ice sheet was the Wisconsin Glaciation. It developed about 100,000 years ago - a blink of the eye in geological terms - and entombed our area and most of the country under great depths of slowly moving ice for tens of thousands of years. The crushing weight and abrasive power of the rock and gravel carried along by the ice scoured the landscape, scraping away softer rocks and loose materials as well as the remnants of the mountains (2). A great deal of material was moved. Even today gneissic and granitic boulders that were carried by the ice sheet can be found stranded on limestone and sandstone bedrock in the lowlands of the Ottawa Valley (5,16, 19). So great was the weight of this ice that the land was depressed several hundred meters. That had important implications for the Capital area at a later date.

Sand and gravel from areas to the north (the direction from which the glacial ice sheet advanced) were deposited throughout the area (2d, 8, 16, 22, 23). They were subsequently reworked and altered by water immediately following the glacial period.

The land in this part of North America began to emerge from the cover of glacial ice about 12,000 years ago. As new accumulations of snow were not making up for the summer melting at the source of the glacier, the leading edge of the ice slowly began to disintegrate. A vast, cold, freshwater lake formed along the front of the ice sheet for the first few centuries because drainage routes were blocked by ice. When a drainage channel was finally released the downward pressure of the ice had been so great that the eastern ocean flowed into the resultant depression. This was the Champlain Sea, of prime importance in forming the landscape in much of the Ottawa Valley.

## The Champlain Sea

At its peak about 11,500 years ago the Champlain Sea stretched along the Ottawa Valley west to Pembroke, north along the Gatineau Valley to about Low and southward across the lowlands to about Smiths Falls. It was cold and deep; fossil remains indicate an arctic-subarctic environment. It seems hard to comprehend but there is little doubt that Bowhead Whales and Ringed Seals once fed along the leads in pack-ice a hundred meters above the present day Peace Tower of the Parliament Buildings with other sea creatures typical of today's northern ocean waters.

Into this northern sea fell a steady rain of microscopic particles that built up along the sea floor and formed a silty ooze. To this were added the remains of plants and animals. With time the silty ooze consolidated to form clay and fragments of some organisms were encapsulated in lumps (or nodules). In a few places in the Capital such fossil-bearing clay nodules are common, providing important evidence of past environments (26). The marine clay of the Champlain Sea is widespread in the Ottawa area and along the north shore of the Ottawa River (15, 17, 22, 26, 28). Sand deposits associated with shoals and near-shore slopes also occur extensively in the Capital (4, 12, 24, 29).

As the land rebounded from the weight of glacial ice over the following centuries (a process that is *still* going on), the sea became shallower. The increased volume of melting glacial ice also freshened the margins of the sea and the flora and fauna adapted accordingly. The Bowhead Whales and Ringed Seals were replaced by Belugas and Harbour Seals as the waters became warmer and less saline.

While all these changes were occurring *in* the sea, associated biological changes were occurring around it. Arctic tundra initially covered the seaside landscape, likely with a complement of northern animals like Arctic Hare, Caribou, Arctic Tern, Caribou and even Polar Bear. Relicts from these prehistoric environments persist on cliff ledges and in other sites where modern vegetation and animal life has been unable to displace organisms that became established thousands of years ago. Subarctic plants on cliffs (2b, 2c) and a land-locked population of sea-going Three-spined Stickleback (2) are examples of this from the Gatineau Hills.

197

About 10,000 years ago the Champlain Sea became very shallow near its mouth and its connection with the eastern ocean was all but cut off. All drainage from the immense Great Lakes basin flowed along the Ottawa Valley (a prehistoric St. Lawrence River, if you will), bringing with it vast amounts of sediment and fresh water into this declining sea. With no inflow of marine water and the tremendous flushing effect of the western fresh water, the marine period in the Ottawa Valley came rapidly to an end.

## The Modern Landscape

While the Champlain Sea may have been gone after two thousand years, the Capital area was still under water. The massive flow of water along the Ottawa Valley brought huge loads of sand with it which were deposited as the river emptied into the shallow former sea basin. These sediments were also reworked locally by the river and lake currents and are in evidence throughout the Capital today (4, 7, 13, 15, 28, 30).By about 9000 years ago the first land in what is now the Regional Municipality of Ottawa-Carleton was emerging from the freshening water (12). With a cool, subarctic climate still present, though perhaps less intense with the glaciers now a couple of hundred kilometers to the north , a vegetation more typical of forested areas in northern Ontario and Quebec today would have been dominant here. As the climate became warmer more and more plants and animals would have migrated from southern areas where they had persisted throughout the glacial period. Others would have migrated along the great river flowing eastward from the Great Lakes basin. A mixture of plants and animals from this period can still be found in relict sites that include former islands in this cool, post-glacial lake (12) .

While the fresh-water lake (called Lake Lampsilis) was entering its later stages as the land continued to rise, the climate became increasingly warm. For several thousand years, from about 8000 years ago when Lake Lampsilis ended to about 5000 or 6000 years ago, the Capital and much of eastern Canada were exposed to a warmer and drier climate than we have today. The northern organisms would have all but died out during this warm period (called the hypsithermal), giving way to immigrants from the south that were better adapted to the new conditions. A landscape of enlarging islands slowly merging into larger land masses developed through this transition period.  Through the western, eastern and southern avenues for floral and faunal migration, boreal, prairie and southern influences were all felt. Remnants of such flora and fauna can still be found at sites throughout the area (2b, 8, 10, 12, 13, 27, 28).

When the warm period ended about 5000 years ago it brought to a close a complex period of change and evolution in the local landscape.  On a geological time scale these changes would have seemed to occur at a frantic pace, happening in only 4000 or 5000 years. The last part of this story was the diversion of the Great Lakes drainage southward through the St. Lawrence Valley about 4000 years ago, thus bypassing the Ottawa Valley. Our landscape was then formed.

The contemporary landscape is a direct product of its past.  So it is that we have huge bogs in abandoned river channels that reflect boreal conditions (28), extensive sand deposits from the shores of long gone seas that have been worked into dunes (13, 20) and ancient, weathered outcrops that are the roots of primeval mountain ranges (1,2,8,14). All of these combine to present the mosaic of landforms and habitats in which plants and animals today strive for success.

# Selected Bibliography

The literature of the geology, geomorphology and post-glacial landscape development of Canada's Capital is immense. I have tried to summarize the major elements and to present them in an easily readable manner. For more detailed and exact information on these topics, however, a number of useful references are listed below. These are in addition to those in the individual site descriptions in the Places to See section.

**Evolution of the Land**
Douglas, R.J.W.(Editor). 1970. Geology and Economic Minerals of Canada. Economic Geology Report 1, Department of Energy, Mines and Resources, Ottawa.

Hogarth, D.D. 1962. A Guide to the Geology of the Gatineau - Lievre District. Canadian Field-Naturalist 76:1-55.

Wilson, A.E. 1956. A Guide to the Geology of the Ottawa District. Canadian Field-Naturalist 70:1-68.

**Glaciation**
Chapman, L.J. and D.F. Putnam. 1966. The Physiography of Southern Ontario. (Second Edition). University of Toronto Press, Toronto.

Prest, V. K. 1970. Quaternary Geology in Canada, *in*, Douglas (see reference in Evolution of the Land, above).

**The Champlain Sea**
Harington, C.R. 1971. The Champlain Sea and its Vertebrate Fauna, Part I. Trail & Landscape 5:137-141.

Harington, C.R. 1972. The Champlain Sea and its Vertebrate Fauna, Part II. Trail & Landscape 6:33-39.

Harington, C.R. 1981. Whales and Seals of the Champlain Sea. Trail & Landscape 15:32-47.

McAllister, D.E. & B.W. Coad. 1974. Fishes of Canada's National Capital Region. Special Publication 24, Department of the Environment, Ottawa.

**The Modern Landscape**
McAllister, D.E. & B.W. Coad. 1974. Fishes of Canada's National Capital Region. Special Publication 24, Department of the Environment, Ottawa.

Brunton, D.F. 1984. Nature Reserve Potential and Management in the National Capital Region on NCC Lands, Ontario/Quebec. Conservation Studies 29, National Capital Commission, Ottawa.

# INDEX

The following lists the places, plants and animals treated in this book. Numbers in bold face indicate the page at which the major treatment of the subject is to be found.

# PLACES T

1 - Poltimore Road
2 - Gatineau Park
  2a - Ramsay Lake
  2b - Eardley Escarpm
  2c - Champlain Looko
  2d - Mackenzie King E
  2e - Old Chelsea Ravi
  2f - Hickory Trail
3 - Wychwood
4 - Champlain Park Woo
5 - Brebeuf Park
6 - Tache Gardens Woo
7 - Leamy Lake Park
8 - Beauchamp Lake Pa
9 - McLaurin Bay
10 - Carleton Place Hackberry Stand
11 - Mill of Kintail Conservation Area
12 - The Burnt Lands

28 - Mer Bleue Conservation Area
29 - Pine Grove
30 - Cobb's Lake

*SEE MAP OPPOSITE PAGE*